MY NAME IS CHARLEY

AN ADVENTUROUS WELSH TERRIER

By

MARJOLYN POLS

This book is a work of fiction. Places, events, and situations in this story are purely fictional. Any resemblance to actual persons, living or dead, is coincidental.

ISBN: 1-4033-8180-1 (e-book)
ISBN: 1-4033-8181-X (Paperback)

This book is printed on acid free paper.

1stBooks - rev. 10/18/02

MY NAME IS CHARLEY

(an adventurous Welsh terrier)

Charley's Signature

Told by: Charley
Written down by: Marjolyn Pols

Contents

Introduction..ix

Charley's vocabulary:..xiii

A special day...1

All alone 10

The pet doctor 12

The Joy-Cat 15

Many, many persons 18

Jack and Jack... 24

Car... 27

The woods.. 31

My house.. 36

Staying some nights out 39

My day 44

The dog school 53

The Mouse... 59

Tara 62

Cocktails.. 65

The day of the trimming 68

The apple and the ball.. 72

The contest.. 75

A birthday party 79

The stick.. 83

Charley and Cooper... 87

Swimming party 92

Cleaning 94

The dishes.. 97

Snow.. 99

The pet hotel 102

My own swimming pool 105

Bowie 108

Many Welsh Terriers..113

Not so good Charley 118

Find...122

A new trimming place..124
The bath...128
And Car again.... 131
Tennis 136
Football 138
Tara's house 140
Letgo..143
The observation post..147
The thief...151
Abroad 154
Salt water 159
My things..163
Eating with a fork..165
Charley's favorite recipes 169
My dictionary 172

Charley Pols, that's me

Introduction

When we had to put to sleep our Great Dane Ludo, the circumstances were such that we could not immediately consider having another dog.

We still were in the happy possession of two Siamese cats, one of which, Byou, of an advanced age, and it would have been unwise to spoil her last few years with the presence of a lively puppy.

In May 1998, however, we had to take our leave from Byou as well and at that moment our house became a very quiet place. Besides that, her pal Joy, was terribly sad and cried the whole day.

We were getting used to our easy life. No more compulsory outings in the rain. No hurrying home to be in time for the dog's outing. Nevertheless we decided that the time had come to have another dog, although at the same time we thought that it would be better not having such a big one anymore, but a smaller breed would do as well. The type, as I still call it, of a carry along dog.

Preferably a breed that is not subject to over breeding (and regretfully there is a lot of over breeding and mismanagement in this respect). Beagle, Kooiker dog and some other breeds were thoroughly scrutinized and after careful consideration, the choice was made for a French bulldog, notwithstanding the long waiting lists.

Although my sister Karen cried that she could not understand what made us choose for this type of dog with the decided look of having walked with his snout into a brick wall, we remained firm in our belief that the French Bulldog would be our best choice.

A Sunday visit to Marjolyn (yes another one) and Dick Langwerden, to finally see their redecorated and partially rebuilt farmhouse, provided an agreeable surprise. A Welsh terrier, called Tara, warmly welcomed us and when we learnt in the course of our conversation with Tara's bosses that Tara was in the family way, we were immediately sold to the idea of a Welsh.

Quite elated we drove back home. A couple of days later, however, we were bitterly disappointed to learn that Tara was not pregnant at all. Our nice plans were really double-crossed.

In the mean time we were absolutely and totally focused on a Welsh terrier so that we (read: Bill) made an enormous amount of phone calls to breeders. No Welsh available. Not for many weeks at least.

There was just one five months old puppy available from a breeder in the south of the country. He originally had wanted to keep the pup for himself, but due to special family circumstances the pup had to be given away.

There was one little snake in the grass: a holiday trip that could not be cancelled at such a short notice. A quick phone call to Karen and Hans was enough and the pup was very welcome during our holidays.

Full of expectation we drove southwards ……….. and Charley himself tells the rest of the story.

Marjolyn Pols

Charley's vocabulary:

Bill	My number one boss, my own manperson
Marjolyn	My number two boss, my own womanperson
House	My own bench, an inside territory
Woods	The place with many trees to have walks
Along	Does not matter whereto, as long as I can come along
Out	Being or going outdoors
Sit	Squat
Down	Flat on the ground
Let go	Something I almost always refuse to do
Car	The shiny beast that takes us everywhere
Joy	My own cat
Uran	One of my friends (a dog)
Karen	Hugperson
Hans	Manperson, who lives in the same territory as the hugperson
Cooper	The hugpersons' dog

Bowie	Has lived in our territory for some time
Come	To approach Bill
Come here	To approach and remain there in front of him
Stay	And continue to be there
Food	The best thing that can happen
Cookie	Deeelicioussss
Treat	Also very deeeeliciousss
No	Not allowed
Blacknose	No idea. Does that belong to me?
For shame	Something very wrong
Easy	Don't grasp to fast or don't jump to fast on the sleeping place of Bill and Marjolyn
Rope	My favorite toy
Ball	Also quite nice
Nice	When I have been trimmed
Stick	Toy in the woods
Good boy	At least ten times a day
To bed	Close my eyes to sleep
Drink	Lap from my dish
Watch me	To look Bill in the eyes

A special day

It was quite clear to me this morning. This was to be a very special day. Not a day like all the other days. A day of getting up in the morning and kick up a dust with my sister Hetty. Bark and bark until our manperson comes to feed us.

The new persons came when I had been playing with my ball for a very long time. They liked it a lot to see me jumping as high as I could and they took me for some outdoor rounds just to see if I would behave nicely walking on a leash.

There are many big beasts in the outside territory. They don't have hair and they are quite shiny.

They don't have paws to walk on but round things, rolling them forward. In the beginning I was a bit scared because they make a lot of noise. My manperson held me on a tight leash, so that nothing could happen to me and they could not approach me.

I have seen many shiny beasts now and I am no longer afraid. I keep my tail upright, as it should be.

1

Many other big and small persons are to be seen outside our territory. Sometimes they walk, sometimes they sit on a thing and they move their paws up and down. I like to try and grasp their paws with my teeth, but my manperson does not allow it.

He calls shame on me!

The new persons are walking with us. They are a manperson and a womanperson as far as I can understand. I do the best I can and do not pull on the leash. My manperson doesn't want that. When I do that he talks to me with a very dark voice.

The new persons talk to my manperson. I don't know exactly what about, but it gives me a strange feeling. When we are back in our territory I am not going back in the small territory with Hetty.

No, it isn't funny, because I am taken to the small house. The small house has a table in it and I have to stand on that table.

My own manperson ties me up and starts to comb my snout. I do not like that at all, but it isn't half as bad as trimming. Something awful that he has done to me already a couple of times and it hurts. I don't like trimming.

The new persons caress me and that is something I do like. The womanperson does not have a dark voice and she says things that make me feel quite good. Although I have not the faintest idea what she means.

They leave and I am sent back to the small territory with Hetty. We are alone again. What a pity. I jump high a couple of times, but they do not come back. Okay, let us play ball again for a while.

The door opens and my manperson enters. He picks me up and carries me to a place I have never seen before. It is not very far away. The new persons are also there. The womanperson puts a collar around my neck and a leash. It is not the one I usually carry.

She lifts me and carries me right to a shiny beast. The shiny beast is quiet and stands still. The new manperson is already sitting inside the shiny beast and they put me there as well.

This is not so good and the only consolation is that I am sitting very close to the new womanperson. She holds me tight.

The shiny beast starts to growl and I am still in his inside, but I am a Welsh and that means that you have to behave like one. Or shouldn't I?

The manperson is the boss of the shiny beast and that is why he doesn't do anything wrong and behaves himself properly.

He continues to growl but no further action except that he starts to move.

It takes a very long time and I start to have a strange feeling in my belly. I am going to throw up, I am quite sure. The shiny beast stands still and stops growling. The womanperson takes me out and the manperson is cleaning the insides of the shiny beast. I am in a very strange place. Everything smells strange and new. There is street and there is grass. Not much more. Also a large box. The box smells with many different smells, some good some bad. I would like to have a look inside this box, but the womanperson doesn't allow it. She says the same word many times: "No, no, no".

So˙I think that No means no good.

The womanperson talks to me again. It sounds good, but let us face it I do not understand a word of it. I think I am going to pee.

We are back in the insides of the shiny beast. He starts to growl again. I am sitting close to the womanperson and the persons are talking together. All of a sudden I hear my name: Fitus. I look up at the womanperson and she wants me to continue looking at her, I can feel that. She says the same word many times: "Charley, Charley, Charley". Many times again and she looks at me.

Am I Charley? And no longer Fitus?

I have to throw up my food again. I don't like any of this. I feel bad. The shiny beast continues to growl. I would like to go back to my own manperson and Hetty.

The shiny beast stands still and has stopped growling. Did we go back perhaps?

The manperson picks me up and he puts me down in a place I don't know. It smells with a strange smell. I can smell the smell of the new persons. This is their territory. I can also smell another animal. I do not know what type. I cannot see him.

The manperson puts me down on a soft place. That feels good. There is a ball. It isn't mine, but when I chew carefully on it, it will become mine. There is also a dish and there is water in it. The dish has no smell. I start to taste the water and it tastes good. I lap it up so that the dish smells like my dish and the water becomes my water.

I get up and the womanperson calls me with my new name: "Charley, Charley". I think I am going to walk around a bit to have a good look at this place. Everything is new and everything smells different. The territory is small and at the end some thing is in the way and closes off the territory.

I cannot see what the situation is on the other side. I have to stand upright to have a look. On the other side I can see the new persons and they are looking at me and they talk to me as well. It sounds good, but even better is that the womanperson now gets a small box and in that box there is something that smells very good. She gives the something to me. I like that taste. Very, very much.

"Cookie, cookie", is what she says. I got it: the nice smelling something is cookie! Something to remember carefully.

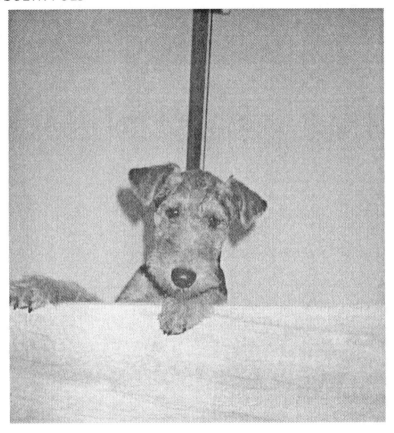

Charley in his small territory

I have seen quite a few new things and drop down on the soft place. Do you think that my own manperson will come? And do I have to return inside the shiny beast? I have to pee and sit in a corner of the territory. O wow, that is all wrong because the womanperson comes running towards me and says: "No, no". She picks me up and puts my collar and leash on. Are we going home now?

We are walking in a street. It isn't my street. I am allowed to sniff around and when I start to pee again, the womanperson says: "Good boy, good boy".

Many times the same word and with a light voice. Good boy is good and therefore to pee means to be a good boy.

All alone

The manperson puts me down on the soft place again. It is getting dark and there are only a few noises. I don't like it very much. I feel like crying a little bit. Then the light is on again. The manperson has come back and he talks to me with a friendly voice. He picks up the box with the cookies. So, I understand that if I cry I get a cookie. Also something to remember.

The manperson leaves again and it is dark again. I start to cry, because that may help, but after all it doesn't. So to cry doesn't mean a cookie at all.

I am going to sleep, because all these happenings have made me quite tired.

When I wake up, it is still dark. I get up. I have to pee, but I cannot go to the outside place. Okay, let us go into a corner. I don't like it too much to pee in my new territory. That isn't the thing to do.

I am going to sleep again and when I wake up this time the light is on. The manperson has come into the territory and talks to me. He puts my collar and leash on. I stay down, because I have not the slightest wish to go outside. The manperson carries me and puts me down on the street. So what, I can sit down again.

The manperson picks me up again and we go a few steps ahead. He puts me down in the grass and wow the grass is very wet. I hate to sit in the wet grass. Okay, you win, let's walk.

That day I have to go outside many times, sometimes with the manperson, sometimes with the womanperson. I have no other "little accidents" in my territory.

I think that we are going outside a lot of times and I cannot say that I like it all the time, but it is nice that after every trip I get my treat when we are back in our territory.

Sometimes just a cookie, but sometimes a dish with good food. A lot of good food. The same food as in my old territory, but in those days I never had cookies.

The pet doctor

Today, after our first outing, the manperson carries me into the shiny beast. I keep my paws straight to offer some resistance, because I don't like to be in the insides of the shiny beast. The womanperson also sits in the beast and holds me tight. The beast starts growling. For some time all is well and I do not have to throw up.

It doesn't take too much time and then the beast stops growling and stands still again.

We leave the beast and we are in a place I have never seen before. We enter a territory, but it is a strange territory because it smells like many animals. All of them different types. There are dogs like me, but they have different colors. Some of them are ready to touch nose, some of them don't like that. They make a lot of noise and bark and growl. I am not yet able to bark but I would love to learn it.

I am being taken to yet another place. There is a manperson and a table. Wow, I think, this means trimming again and I have no wish at all to do that. But this manperson just looks into my ears and in my mouth and he touches every spot of my body. He puts a pin in my backside, but that doesn't hurt too much. And that is already better than I expected, because he doesn't do any trimming. He talks to my womanperson, but as usual I have no idea what they are talking about. It is really a pity that I don't understand this personlanguage. I would love to know what they are saying. Shall I ever learn?

My manperson picks me up again and puts me on the ground. The other manperson gives me a cookie. Well, that is quite an agreeable surprise. We are going back to the shiny beast and my manperson carries a big bag of nice smelling food. The manperson of the table gave it to him. The big bag comes with us. Can it be for me?

The shiny beast takes us to our own territory. I am happy to be back.

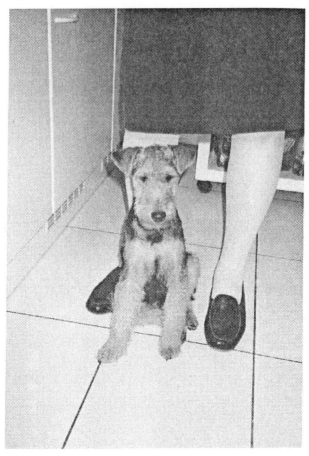

Charley is glad to be back in his territory

The Joy-Cat

When I am back in our territory after quite a few outings, I stand upright against the thing that divides my small territory from the rest of the large territory. I cannot get across, but at least I can see what happens on the other side. All the time I can smell that other animal, but I have not yet seen him. The womanperson arrives and she calls me: " Charley, Charley". I look up and then all of a sudden I see the animal. It is not a dog like me, but I think that I have seen such an animal before. I cannot remember if I can trust it, because in my memory it was not so good.

This animal belongs in our territory, as far as I can smell. The womanperson says: "Cat, cat, cat". I have certainly heard that word before. Is that the animal?

The animal looks at me and makes a sound that I cannot recognize. The womanperson takes away the thing so that I can walk into the larger territory. The animal retreats into the territory. Is he afraid of me? He lifts his paw. I get the smell of his paw and then he runs away very quickly. I follow him immediately. This seems like quite a nice game after all.

He is hiding. Okay, never mind, because I can smell you. So let us get there. The womanperson calls again: "Cat, cat, cat". Aha, that means that the animal is called Cat. Cat is coming out of his hiding place and looks at me. He doesn't run away anymore, so I just look at him. One never knows and I prefer to be careful. Cat is sniffing at my paws. Quite a situation, but all is well and nothing happens. Finally he puts his tail in an upright position and slowly turns around.

The womanperson picks up Cat and shows him to me and then she says: "Joy, Joy, Joy". Is Cat Joy or Cat?

I think it is like this: I am Welsh and they call me Charley and the animal is Cat and they call him Joy.

I am quite tired. I am going to have a little nap.

Charley and Joy

Many, many persons

The next couple of days I am very busy. Many outdoors trips. Many times a day, because from time to time I still have "little accidents" in our territory. In the meantime Joy and me have become the best possible friends. I have discovered that she is a womancat. She loves me a lot and frankly speaking, I like her too. We have many romps, but she always wins, because she is very clever. She hides out somewhere in a very high place, so that I cannot reach her.

But I can be clever too, because I choose a position that makes it impossible for her to go somewhere else and I am patient. Sometimes, however, it takes so long that I am fed up and then, of course, I leave the scene.

Today I can feel, is a different day. The persons are behaving in a different way. They walk around quite a lot and seem to be busy with many things. They hardly look at me.

All of a sudden there is a noise that I have never heard before, a sort of buzzing.

The womanperson walks to the door that we never use when we go outdoors and she opens it.

Wow, this is great fun, a lot of persons are coming into our territory. I jump as high as I can to say hello to them all and they are behaving very friendly. I hear my name many times.

They give me a paper, but there is something inside that paper. This really is great fun. The smell is terrific. I rip the paper away and I am left with a thing that I don't know at all, but I would love to eat it, because of its smell, which is as good as I have never smelled before.

I take it along to my soft place and start eating. That is not so easy, because it is a very tough thing and it takes me a long time to eat it. I cannot even break it into small pieces and strangely enough the taste remains okay. Well, what can I do but continue to chew on it.

The new persons stay a long time and I am allowed to stay with them. I have hidden myself under the table where the persons always have their food. I have understood in the meantime that persons don't eat from their dish like me, but from a table. So a table is not only for trimming. To be under the table is like being in a hole and when I am in hiding the paws of the persons are the only things I can see. It is nice to lie down on the paws on my manperson. I can close my eyes and at the same time I know that he is still there.

When it is light again, other new persons arrive. They are not the same new persons. These new persons are big and small. The small persons like it a lot that I can jump as high as I do. They brought me some treats. I unwrap them all. No problem. One of the papers contains a ball. It makes a curious noise. When I chew the ball it howls. Well, that means that I have to continue chewing, because that is the best solution to keep it howling. I can even take the ball to our outdoor territory.

Yes, indeed, we have an outdoor territory of our own as well. I know the difference because in our own outside territory I am not supposed to pee. The first time when I was there and I did that, the manperson loudly called shame on me and his voice was very dark.

I never do it again because I don't like it at all when my persons are angry at me.

Yet a new group of persons is coming. They pick me up. They also like me, but this time I can jump and jump, but regretfully I get no package. So just to justify my jumping activity I jump high enough to get the package of my womanperson. The package contains flowers, with long streamers and those are absolutely interesting to chew on.

On the next day other new persons are arriving and we are going to sit outdoors, since it is a very hot day. I had been in the shadow with the Joy-Cat the whole day. I like the sun but this was too much. Even my soft place has been brought outdoors, so that I can lie down on it from time to time.

The persons who are visiting us must feel warm as well, because they are all sitting in the shadow on a bench next to my own persons. Close to the bench there are some trees with good-looking twigs. I take a bite, but the taste is awful and immediately my manperson gets up and he opens my mouth and pulls out all the twigs I tried to eat. He is very angry and throws much water into my mouth to take the bad taste away.

There is much shame on me, I can tell.

Charley and Joy outdoors

I run to lie down on my soft place. It will pass. After all, I do not think it was a good idea to eat these twigs. And besides that, they certainly tasted awful.

All new persons who come to visit are leaving us, but fortunately my own persons remain in our territory. When the new persons arrive they always call my persons with the same word. I have listened very carefully and that is why I now know that my womanperson is called Marjolyn and my manperson is

Bill. I have to keep that in mind. I have a lot of things on my

mind anyhow. It is quite tiring, you know.

Jack and Jack

On a day some other new persons arrive. It is still very warm outdoors and instead of having the food from the indoor table, like the persons do, they now eat from an outdoor table. The food is not prepared in the usual area where the food is always prepared, an area that I call the makefoodplace, but there is this thing carried outdoors by my manperson and it makes smoke and fire. Very interesting and exciting. The special buzzing sound is there and I now know that it warns us about the arrival of the new persons. Who is coming today? I have met so many persons now and they gave me many presents. Let me see what happens today.

There are two manpersons and I do not know them at all. They are very friendly to me, but they do not have a package with paper. Too bad.

We are outdoors now. I am positioning myself under the outdoor table so that I can have a close look at what is happening.

Some treats are brought out of the indoor territory and put on the fire and smoke thing. I want to have a closer look and standing upright enables me to see what happens. Absolutely the wrong decision, because the shame is on me again! The fire and smoke thing is quite hot and much too hot for my paws. So under the table is the best place to be for wait and see. I think that today is a day of wait and see.

The new manpersons talk to my own persons and my name is mentioned many times. What a disaster that personlanguage, because I still miss a lot of the interesting discussions.

I have to present myself at the table because they are eating and I think they are forgetting about me. I have to do something about that and I can tell you that in the meantime I have understood that if I sit in front of the persons and look in a way as if I have not had a decent meal in many days, it always helps to get some treat.

I select one of the new manpersons. He has a light voice, so he must be a friendly person.

It works, it works I get my treat.

Marjolyn has seen it, but she does not make a dark voice this time. So far, so good.

Bill is still busy with the smoke and fire thing. Again some treats are coming to the table and Marjolyn calls the new manpersons. First one and then the other. They also have a name but they have both the same name. How curious. They are both called Jack.

I absolutely do not understand this. Just imagine that there would be another Welsh and his name would also be Charley. It would be so very confusing if Bill would call me. How would I know that he talks to me?

Strange personways.

Although after all it is no problem for me, because I know who is who, because I can always smell it and apart from that I recognize the personvoices.

I go back to my safe place underneath the table. I can relax and I do not have to think about all those complicated personthings.

Car

One day Marjolyn picks me up and we go outdoors again. Wow, this is wrong, we are going inside the shiny beast.

"Car, Car", says Marjolyn. Is the shiny beast called Car? I hate to go inside, because it makes me throw up my food. This time I am not sitting close to Marjolyn, but I am dumped on the ground, very low. I do not like it one little bit. It is creepy. I cannot see anything at all. I have no idea where we are going. But whatever I do, I just have to stay in that position.

Well, maybe it is for the best, because one thing is true I don't feel the need to throw up my food. Car stops moving and growling. I jump up. I want out. My collar and leash are put on and we are leaving Car. Marjolyn and I are going for a walk. It is a new and unknown outdoor territory. There are many unknown things and big and small persons. We are even going to enter a new indoor territory. That is great fun, because it is a place full of treats that I would like to eat, and also balls and other toys I have never seen before. But above all there are many unreal animals with nice smells. They look like animals, but they only move when you take them in your mouth and shake them.

Marjolyn is picking up many treats. I want to help her and pick something up as well. I grasp one of the unreal animals and that is not allowed. Shame on me again! But I am not a fool. It is far too nice to let go, so I fix my teeth around it. Marjolyn is angry and makes a dark voice with much growl and I can even see her teeth. Okay I will let it go, but what a great pity. The unreal animals don't join us, but many of the other treats are coming with us.

We are walking back for a while and then suddenly I can see Car. I can smell that it is Car, because he smells in a different way than the other shiny beasts. He smells like our territory. Besides that I can recognize his voice when he is growling.

Car takes us back to our territory. Since I am now better acquainted with Car, I do not dislike him anymore.

Charley and Car

It is even nice to be inside Car, because we are all together and it seems very safe, because nobody can get us when we are inside Car.

When we are back in our territory I am given one of the new treats. It is a big thing. I can take it in my mouth. Bill wants to take it back from me, but I simply cannot let this happen. This thing is mine now and I don't let it go. It is too much fun. He pulls and pulls, but I don't let it go. Let us see who is the strongest. Bill says: "Let go, let go". Can it be that the thing is called Letgo? I give Letgo to Bill and he throws it away. I run to get Letgo again. I bring Letgo to Bill and we continue our game. We both pull and I decide to make a growling noise. It certainly may help to scare Bill away. Do I really want to scare Bill away? No, but I do this as a game and that is not serious. Marjolyn brings me a cookie. I drop Letgo, because I like him a lot but I like my cookie better.

"Good boy", says Marjolyn. Why is that? What did I do to be praised?

I am quite tired. I think I need a little nap. I walk off to my soft place.

The woods

Today we are going outside again. But, instead of our usual rounds, we are walking into another direction. There is no street but only grass and sand and there are many big and small trees. Bill has taken our ball with him. He has hidden the ball, but don't kid me I can always smell it. I can smell it immediately, because it is my ball that I have chewed carefully and many times. So I jump and jump as high as I can, hoping that he understands that I want my ball. Something special is happening, because my collar is taken off and all of a sudden I can walk and run wherever I want to go and all by myself. I run and run. Bill calls my name. What can that mean? I look at him, but I do not approach him too closely to avoid him putting my collar on again. I like being without my collar and leash. It makes me feel free to do as I please.

Bill turns around and walks into another direction. I have to pay attention to that, because I do not like to be left all alone, since I would not know what to do. So I shall keep my distance but pay careful attention that he remains in sight.

Bill throws the ball in my direction. That is good work. I get it and drop down with it. That is better that to remain standing up. I chew the ball thoroughly, which makes it even a lot more mine.

Suddenly Bill grasps the ball and takes it from me. I have no idea what he is going to do. He throws the ball away. Really a long distance. I run after it. This starts to be a very nice game. So that's why I bring the ball back and fortunately Bill understands my meaning, because he throws it away again. We do this many times.

Bill now puts the ball high up in a tree, between the branches. I jump high to get it, but I cannot reach it. I can assure you that next time when we go to the woods I shall know where to find it. I shall walk straight towards this tree to show Bill where he left the ball. He can pick it out of the tree and we can continue our game.

The game doesn't take long, because there are some new persons in the woods. Not just persons, but also a dog. The dog doesn't look like the Joy-Cat or me. He is quite big, but he seems friendly and wags his tail a lot. That 's why I know that he is friendly. He approaches me and I move my tail as well, so that he can see that I am a friendly dog. I cannot wag my tail, because I do not have that type of tail. We are running around very fast together. He runs a lot faster that I do, because he is much bigger. He is young like me and loves to play. Another new person is arriving. He also has a dog. This is a nice place to be. The new dog approaches us too. He doesn't wag his tail very much. He seems to be quite old and doesn't want to play. I lie down on my back to show him that I have good intentions. He is sniffing me and turns around.

He doesn't stay with us. My new friend is called Uran and every time we meet, we play a lot together and we run around. He still runs a lot faster that I but I have invented a trick. I make some short cuts, so that after all I can keep up with him quite well.

Charley in the woods

If we go to the woods often, I shall make many new

friends. There are some other nice dogs, also a very wild one,

she is called Cajsa and then there are two from the same

family, but they don't want to play. They are called Annick and

Jenny and they have very long hair.

My house

On a certain day Marjolyn is coming back into our territory with a very large package. I always want to know everything, so I jump up immediately to see what this is about. It is something very new. Marjolyn and Bill unwrap it. I still don't understand what is inside this package. It grows. At first it was low and flat; now it has another shape. Marjolyn takes away my soft place. The new thing is put down on the spot of my soft place and my soft place is put inside this thing. I must have a look and enter the thing and lie down on my soft place. The thing has a small door that can be opened and closed. Bill closes the door. It is nice in a way, because I am on my soft place, but nobody can reach me and at the same time I can see everything. I can use my snout to push against the door and I can leave. I return quickly to take possession of my new place.

Marjolyn says: " House".

Is the thing House? I like House a lot. House is mine. Nobody else can enter. The Joy-Cat comes to have a look. She is so small and walks into my House just like that. I think she likes my House too. I like her so she is allowed into my House. She doesn't stay long and leaves.

Joy-Cat has a place of her own after all.

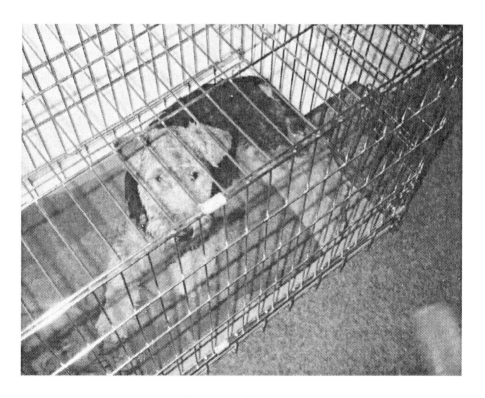

Charley in his House

I am very happy with my House and sit or lie in it as often as I can. When it is dark and we have made our rounds, Marjolyn says: "Charley, to bed". I get my cookie and my dish with water and I stay in my House.

The door is closed, the dark comes and I can sleep comfortably.

Before I had my House, I sometimes got up in the dark to pee in our territory, but since I have my House I don't do that anymore. I don't want to pee in my own House. That's very wrong. So now I really have to wait till daylight and Bill or Marjolyn comes to get me for a walk outdoors.

Staying some nights out

Today some other new persons are coming to see us. They hug my persons and they are very friendly to me. The new womanperson takes me to the woods and we take a long walk. We go back to our territory and when the persons are inside I can also come with them. I jump on the lap of the new womanperson and hug her. She makes some noises, but I can feel that she likes it. This is what I do to hug: I jump on her lap and hold her tightly with my forepaws and than hug hug hug thoroughly.

Bill doesn't allow it many times. He puts me down. I believe that womanpersons like hugging better than manpersons.

After some light and dark times, we leave with Car. I can see that my House is also in Car and my dishes, my treats and my cookies. Even my ball and Letgo are coming along.

What is going to happen?

It is a long way and it takes a long time before Car stops growling and we leave him. We have arrived in a new territory.

Persons are coming towards us and pick up my things. They are persons I know. I like them. It is the womanperson of the hugging.

Marjolyn says: "Charley, this is Karen" and she points out the hugperson. So, the hugperson is called Karen. I start to understand better and better what my persons mean.

We all go into the new territory. I guard my House, because it belongs to me.

I lie down in it, so that nothing can happen.

I hear that Car is growling. What's that supposed to mean? Is Car leaving without me? I run from my House and have a look around. Marjolyn and Bill are not there anymore, but Karen and the manperson who also belongs in their territory are there. At least that is something.

I am going to wait for the return of Marjolyn and Bill. It takes a very long time. Karen is giving me food and treats and drink. I go into my House to sleep.

When the light is on, Karen takes me to a new wood with many trees and sand. I can dig in the sand, but I don't do that, because I don't like it very much. There are many new dogs and many new manpersons and womanpersons in this wood. I am not acquainted with them. They talk about me with Karen. I can feel it.

When we walk back we pass a territory with very strange animals. They are looking more or less like the flying animals in the woods that can sit in a tree. I would like to get at them sometimes, but until now I haven't been successful, because whenever I come close to them they fly away immediately. These new flying animals walk on the ground, just like me. I pull on my leash very hard and Karen lets me go by myself. This means running after the walking flyanimals.

The flyanimals run fast and jump very high, so that they do reach a tree. What a pity. I cannot reach them now. Karen runs towards me and says: "Shame on you"! There is also a new manperson. He comes out of his territory and he is very angry. Karen and the new manperson are both very angry. I keep my tail down, so that they can see that I am sorry.

Karin picks up my leash and we walk away.

When we are back in the territory, Karen says many things. I cannot understand all of it, but I can see that she is still angry.

The manperson, who is in the same territory as Karen, is called Hans and Hans sometimes also takes me for walks in the woods. When it is dark we go together, all three of us. That is also quite funny.

In the territory of Karen and Hans, there is something that we do not have in our territory. It is possible to climb very high. I have tried this out just to have a look what else could be seen in the higher territory. There was a large soft place and it looked good enough for me to take a nap on it. Very pleasant. Suddenly Karen called me from the lower territory. I had to go to her, but when I arrived at the spot where you can go down to the lower territory, I didn't want to continue. It was not as simple to go down as I had thought. I stood there and could not move. Frankly speaking, I was a bit scared and Karen had to come and pick me up. It is now impossible to go to the high place, because there is a sort of door in front of it.

After many dark and light times when I was asleep in my House, I heard some voices. The voices belonged to Marjolyn and Bill and it made me very happy. I opened my eyes and they were standing in front of my House. I left my House immediately and I jumped very very high.

My House and all my other things went back into Car and we went back to our own territory.

I do certainly want to return to Karen and Hans again, but not for such a long time.

By the way, Karen gave me a package. I thought it might be something nice, but it was not nice at all. What a disappointment. It contained a hissing, stinking thing and she sprayed it on my hair. They were laughing at me and they said something, but I don't even want to know what it was. I was not amused. Marjolyn put this thing in my box. I hope they will never take it out again.

My day

When light is back I start to make some noise. I want to get out of my House and do something else. I stretch my back and walk around. Sometimes Bill is coming to get me out, sometimes Marjolyn. Sometimes I have to call them, because when it takes too long before they arrive, I am bored and want out.

Some days it takes a long time before we go out and sometimes we leave immediately.

When I am out of my House and join Bill and Marjolyn, they return to their own soft place and I lie down there as well. Sometimes they are sleeping. If they sleep, I sleep as well. I like it a lot to be asleep all together. The Joy-Cat is there too. She is sleeping long and deep. When it is light she always stays on the soft place of the persons and after that she continues to sleep in another place. When the weather is warm she sleeps in another place than when it's cold. She doesn't go outside very often, but she can go if she likes it. She always walks alone. I am never alone; I am always with my persons.

When it is very cold the Joy-Cat doesn't need to go outside. She has a little box to do her peeing in. Quite comfortable to be cat, because you never need to go outside into the cold. Outside is nice, but sometimes it is very wet and I dislike that particularly. Wet paws and even my belly gets wet.

There is a lot of wet on the street and in the woods. Bill also doesn't like it at all. I can feel that. He doesn't like wet paws and water. Marjolyn doesn't come with us when it is wet. She waits for us and when we return, I have to stay in the small territory and Marjolyn is rubbing me with a towel. Even after the drying I have to stay in the small territory, until I am totally back to normal.

Well whatever, it is very cozy when we are all together in our territory and asleep.

I can stand this for a long time. Later we leave for a walk anyhow, whether it is nice or bad weather.

To return home is also quite nice, because my food is waiting for me in my dish. I always polish off all of it in a hurry, because sometimes the Joy-Cat passes by and she takes a bit from my food. She was in our territory before me, so that is why I am forced to accept this affront, but I cannot quite like it. By the way, her food is always ready in a place that I know to find and if I get the chance to go there I certainly use the opportunity to eat some or all of her food.

Bill and Marjolyn don't allow it and they are very angry when I do it. Shame is in the air again! I can try and look very well as if I am hungry, but it doesn't really work. They just don't believe me.

When I have finished my meal I am going to have a look, to see who is at home. If Marjolyn is at home she will sit in her everyday place and I am joining her. I make believe that I am sleeping, but in the meantime I can follow everything that happens in our territory. If she is not at home I am sitting with Bill, who has another everyday place. Sometimes he is sitting there for a very long time with a big piece of paper in his paws and he is looking at this paper all the time. I don't like that very much and many times I am jumping up and down to make him understand that I would like to play. I take Letgo to him and drop Letgo in front of him. I keep a close look at it, because right when he wants to pick up Letgo I am a little faster than he is.

Sometimes I get my way, sometimes he just doesn't seem to understand. But he is faking that, I am sure. In that case I have to jump even higher and make a lot of effort to achieve my goals.

It also happens from time to time that nobody is home. In that case I have to stay in my small territory and I often sit in my House. Even more fun, it is, to go with Car when I am allowed to come as well. Bill is picking up many things in other territories and sometimes I can go with him. At other times I have to wait inside Car. It just depends on the day. To pick up many things is necessary, because is it food and drink and treats and other things. Sometimes when I am allowed to come along Bill puts me down in a box that can move. In that case I can have a good overview of everything happening around me. The box looks a little bit like my House, but it moves like Car, although it doesn't growl at all. It remains silent, but moves all the same. I stand firmly, because when it moves I don't want to fall out of it.

The things we pick up with the moving box are plants and other things I do not understand.

These are personthings obviously. They smell like nothing and they are no treats and I can do nothing with them.

Even when we do not go with Car, sometimes I have to stay at home all by myself, although I can hear that Bill is in our outside territory. I would love to join him, but it is not allowed.

Once the door to go outside was not closed properly and I was able to go and take a look. I heard Bill somewhere in the outside territory but I did not join him, since I wanted to go and have a look on the street all by myself. I ran towards the street and I saw Rascal passing by with his manperson. Rascal also is a dog but I would not know his type. He has been put together with several types in him. Rascal was on his leash and of course, I was all by myself. Well, as you can imagine I made this known to him with some barking. I don't like Rascal, because he always barks and growls. I have tried that as well and fortunately I am quite good at it of late.

Right when I wanted to pursue him, Bill came running towards me. He called me loudly and his voice was quite angry. He seized me by the scruff of my neck and Rascal has seen it. I was very upset and I felt quite ashamed.

Bill carried me home and dropped me in my territory. I did not get a cookie.

So, let us wait again to see what is going to happen the rest of the day.

Somewhere halfway through the day, we are going to the woods. That's always the longest outing. We make a long walk and go a long distance and today we are going to the grass. There are many big animals walking on the grass. Not dogs and they make a very different noise. They don't bark or growl. They look at me but they don't come near me. They don't even move. Unbelievable, but they eat grass. I like to try that. It does have a strange taste. My own food is much better.

So, I approach these animals and I would like to see what happens then. Could I nose with them? At a close distance they seem to be very big and I change my mind about the nosing. I return to Bill. That seems better.

When we are back in our territory, my food and drink are ready. We still have to wait for some time till Marjolyn returns home. When she arrives, we all stay in our territory in the makefoodplace. Bill and Marjolyn prepare the food they eat themselves. Sometimes I get the opportunity to taste it and that's why I stay there all the time, so that I can closely follow what happens.

Frankly speaking, I love the person food. They have small red balls for example. When I didn't know what they were I played with them for some time and afterwards I have understood that they also could be eaten.

It is quite different from my own food, but absolutely very tasty.

When persons are eating, their dish is not on the ground, but on the table. They also have a place where they can sit. They never sit on the ground, like I do.

If they sit at the table, I go underneath that table and just wait to see if there may be a treat.

Sometimes yes, sometimes no.

When Bill and Marjolyn have finished their meal, they are going to clean their dishes. It is quite curious to see that they never do that with their tongues, because that's what I do with my own dish and it gives my quite some satisfaction. I always polish off until the very last crumb has disappeared and my dish is properly cleaned.

Sometimes it is dark after eating. We all move to another sitting place. In that area there is a box with light and dark flashes and a typical noise. Sometimes a dog barks inside that box. I don't believe it anymore, but the first few times, I shouted back, because frankly speaking, I thought he was coming into my territory.

At other times we move to another place to sit. With a different sort of noise, but no flashes. I love to sit close to Marjolyn and she makes the same noise as from the box. It is a noise that makes me sleepy and many times I listen with my eyes closed.

After some time, we go outside for the last time of the day and then I go into my House for a nice nap. Well, that is my day.

The dog school

On a day when the light has returned and we have had our first outing into the woods, we go inside Car. I have a feeling that something special is going to happen. We are visiting a strange and unknown territory and it is an area with many trees but it has nothing to do with our own woods. There are many new smells and animals as well.

We walk for a while and suddenly I see a large group of dogs. This is great fun. They are all playing together. There are some toys and of course I am participating immediately.

I am free to go and no longer on my leash.

A couple of womanpersons are taking care of us. All the dogs are back on their leashes and one of the womanpersons is starting to talk. Of course, I cannot understand a word of what she says and it seems the same for the other dogs, because they all lie down and probably they think like me: "Well, we'll see what happens".

We are sitting in a large circle and the womanperson is in the middle with a big dog and she says: "Castor, sit". What can this mean? That Castor dog is sitting down and gets a treat. I am interested now. I am eager to know how this works.

The Dog school

The womanperson approaches Bill and me and talks to Bill.

Bill says: "Charley" en then: "Sit". I haven't the faintest idea. I feel slightly foolish and looked at by those other dogs. Do they know? The womanperson now talks to me: "Charley, sit". And while she talks she pushes my tail end down. Okay, let's sit. "Good boy, good boy", says Bill and I get a treat.

We have to do the same thing a lot of times. So mind you: Sit is cookie. There are many words to obtain a cookie …….

Right when I think that I have found out yet another word for cookie, the womanperson approaches us again. She now says: "Charley, watsjfi".

Well what else can I do but look the other way, because it doesn't mean a thing to me?

Again she says: "Charley, watsjfi". She holds my head and if I like it or not, she forces me to look at her. Bill also says: "Charley, watsjfi". I look at him because I think: "Manperson, what do you mean". And guess what he says: "Good boy, good boy".

Yet another cookie. I shall get fat if I go on like this.

I don't really know whether I like all this or not. There are so many things I have to do, which seem quite useless to me, but okay Bill seems to have fun and so I do him a favor and besides that I don't mind at all about all those cookies….

After many light and dark times we return to this new territory with the trees and again the other dogs and the womanpersons are there. The weather is not too good today. Everything is wet, but still I have to sit. It is because Bill says the word and that word means to sit. And let's face it, it also means cookie.

We continue to work and the new word is: Doun. I don't believe this. This seems to mean to go down in the wet grass. I have to think carefully about this. Bill says the doun word a couple of times and finally I decide to drop down, but not because I agree or like it. Oh no.

Again something is happening. Walk around Bill and sit down in front of him. It seems like a funny game. Cookie times again I suppose.

After all I have been to the dog school many times. I have learnt many words and played a lot and especially eaten many cookies.

I now know that Sit means that I have to sit (not always nice in the wet grass). Down means to lie down completely.

56

Stay is to behave like a fool and stay where you are when your manperson walks away. Really an absolutely stupid thing to do.

One of the first few words was watsjfi, but I know better now and it is just the same as: Watch me. And that means looking at Bill and wait until the next word comes. Sometimes the word is Free. That is great fun, because it means that I can go and run wherever I like to run to and do as I please. It is most of the time only for a very short moment, because the next word is: Come. When I hear that word it means that I have to go to Bill. There are moments that I have no great wish to obey and that means that he has to say the come word a couple of times.

Fortunately he is never is really angry. I suppose he thinks that I still have not really understood.

I shall never forget that I had to walk in a long dark bag. It did not seem so great in the beginning, but I am never one to give up easily, so yoho into the bag and no nonsense.

Okay this was a very long bag and yes at the end of the bag Bill was waiting for me with, as you may guess, a cookie.

MARJOLYN POLS

Yes, it really is quite easy, if you do what Bill says, there are many cookies.

The Mouse

One day I walk around in our territory. I am walking around a bit because I do not always want to lie or sit in my House. I jump on the couch, because I have recently discovered, that this enables me to have a good look at what happens outside on the street. It is no big deal, because there is not much traffic in our street with shiny beasts and so on, but from time to time there are some persons or dogs.

I immediately let them know that I live here. It is always wise not to take risks and to take care that no other dogs will enter my territory. Guests are okay but not to stay.

I can hear the Joy-Cat coming into our territory. Sometimes it is difficult to hear her coming in, because she walks very softly. However, I can smell her, so that she cannot surprise me. Look, I am and shall always be a Welsh and Cat is only a cat and you have to keep that in mind.

The Joy-Cat is carrying something in her mouth. I need to know immediately what she has caught. Does she have some treat? I shall take a look.

So I follow her. In the back part of our territory, where she has her soft place, I catch up with her.

She turns around and from her mouth a very small animal drops on the ground. It looks like a very small dog, but it has a different smell. It is real, but not entirely real, because it doesn't move any longer. I think the Joy-Cat hunted it all by herself. Admirable. I have never hunted. Sometimes I see something in the woods, but when I want to run after it, I have to come back immediately. So no chance at all to do some hunting.

The Joy-Cat offers me the little animal. Is this for me? That is really sweet.

Well, it seems like food, so why not try the taste of it. And of course, right on the moment that I have this animal in my mouth, Marjolyn enters the territory. She makes a lot of noise and tries to open my mouth. Well, I am nobody's fool. This animal has been a present and I don't let it go. I know a good solution. I swallow the animal just like that.

It is much to swallow and I cannot say that I like the taste, but once it is yours, you just don't let it go.

Marjolyn is very angry. I think she wanted the animal for herself and maybe I should have given it to her to keep her happy.

I feel that I don't like the animal at all and my belly aches. Very much.

I quickly throw up the animal. Marjolyn picks it up and throws it away in the throwawaythingsbox. It is a big box outside and I cannot look into it. I would like to do that sometimes, but no way. Gone is the little animal.

Joy-Cat has left. She has gone outside. Well, whenever she brings another animal of that kind, I don't want it. Awful!

Tara

Once on a day there are new persons coming to our territory, but this is a very special visit since they also bring a dog along. I am very enthusiastic about it, because she (it is a womandog) looks exactly like me. Besides that she has a present for me. I am getting a new collar and it is identical to the one she wears herself.

It is quite a coincidence since I immediately understand that the womanperson, who is with her, has exactly the same name as my Marjolyn. The manperson is not called Bill, but something different, which I have not understood until now.

The other Marjolyn is very friendly to me and she points out the womandog and says: "Tara, Tara, Tara". And of course, I understand this immediately. The womandog is called Tara.

Tara and I are going to the woods with our persons. I think it is a perfect plan, because now I am able to show everybody who is Tara and Tara can get acquainted with my woods. Tara's manperson keeps her on a long leash. She can walk away for a little stretch, but it is nothing compared with my freedom. I am happy that we don't have such a leash in our house. I have only my normal leash and it is always taken off as soon as we reach the first sitting place in our woods.

When we return in our house we go back into our territory and Tara joins us. We are given some cookies and my Marjolyn gets her flash and continuously flashes Tara and me.

Tara and Charley (left and right)

The persons are eating and we also are having something. I have tasted this before. It is not my usual food, nor one of my cookies. It tastes almost like water and it is quite good. Marjolyn creates it from a long green stick, which she cuts into little pieces.

Marjolyn and Bill eat this as well. So it must be personfood.

When we have eaten everything Tara and her persons are leaving. Tara also has a shiny beast, but it is not like Car. She goes inside and doesn't seem afraid.

I am sorry that Tara is leaving, because now I have to give up my Tara collar. It is put into the box with my other stuff and the hissing thing I got from Karen. Okay, leave it there. Those things I prefer not to see ever again.

Cocktails

When the day goes on, there are some times that Bill and Marjolyn are going to sit in the sitting area. That's always very cozy, because most of the times they are also having food and drink. If it is cold, there is fire in the wall. I have once taken a close look and it was very hot.

Sometimes the warmth is nice, but you cannot touch it with your paws.

I lie on the ground or sit close by.

The Joy-Cat also approaches the fire. She loves the heat too and I can understand that since she has thin hairs.

Bill and Marjolyn are rustling with papers and it takes them a long time to look at them. Fortunately there are drinks and treats in the meantime.

I don't get anything to drink in the sitting area, but every time they have a treat, I get one as well. The person treats are not the same as my own treats. I think that's a pity, because my treats are no surprise at all because they are exactly the same as the food that I get for my dinner.

Other treats are pieces of the green stick or the little red balls.

Since I was of opinion that I must absolutely taste these person treats, once I waited till everybody had left the sitting area. A beautiful moment to position myself on my hind paws close to the table. I could reach everything and I was fully aware of the fact that I had to be quick about it. So I ate all the person treats in one blow. It was rather a mouth full. Not in the least easy to get down fast and of course, when Marjolyn entered the sitting area again, she saw me with my mouth full of stuff.

The biggest problem was that I absolutely could not gobble it up, because there was something inside like a little stick. I really had a problem to get rid of that stick without giving up my earnings. Nowadays I am clever enough to work it out before I start eating this sort of treats. Not at that time. And like always the shame was in the air.

Well, what can I say? It was just to get the taste. Wasn't it??

Another time I had discovered something very special and funny on that table in the sitting area. Many, very sweet tasting little sticks. And those sticks certainly were meant to eat. They were hidden in some paper, but it was no big deal to get rid of that. It was delicious, but not allowed.

Afterwards these delicious sticks had been put on another table, but well, you know, there was a chair close by. I just had to jump on the chair and I could easily eat many more sweet sticks.

After that adventure I did not see the sticks anymore, because Marjolyn hid them someplace else.

The day of the trimming

One day when we come back from our early morning outing, I can see it happen. We are going somewhere with Car. It takes a long time in Car and I am rather curious to know what we are going to do. We arrive in a new territory.

I can see many dogs and they all look exactly like me. That's interesting.

It is someone's territory but I cannot smell whose. A little bit of everybody, like the woods. In the woods I have the continuous problem that I have to show that I have been there, but such things are unthinkable in an inside territory. That is something I understand quite well since some time.

There are many manpersons and womanpersons and tables.

Marjolyn and Bill talk to a manperson and we walk in the direction of one of those tables. They put me on the table and Marjolyn keeps me there. I get this strange feeling. This just might not be as funny as I originally thought.

Well, have you ever, the manperson is starting to trim me. I had not counted on such a cowardly action and I would love to bite him. Of course, no way, so I keep quiet. A bit of growling does no harm, but might be of help. It doesn't.

The trimming takes an awful, awful long time and even Bill starts to trim me. This is not my idea of a nice day, but I stay calm with my usual pluck and spirit.

Moreover, there are many other dogs and some of them are behaving very foolish and they bite and make a lot of noise.

I look at them and try to show them that I am not such a silly one. But I can tell you it is quite an effort to keep up appearances.

After an interminably long time the trimming stops and I think: Aha, we are going home. No, we are going to have a walk outside and return to the inside territory with many other tables.

For a change these tables are full of treats. Not for me, mind you, but for Marjolyn and Bill.

Will they give me something?

No, forget it, it just isn't my day. Not even the smallest possible cookie.

After the feeding of the persons, we go even back to the trimming territory. All dogs are on the tables and of course I have to go too.

I am very very happy that there are no mirrors in this territory, because I would not want to have to see how dreadful I must look now. All my beautiful hairs have gone and if I came here with a bushy tail, there seems to be nothing left of it, right now.

Finally we go back into Car. I am exhausted and take a nap. This was a long, long day. I hate trimming.

The next day I look in the mirror. I can see it, an absolute failure. Bill should never trim me again. That would be much better, but how am I to let him know.

He will never understand that.

After some dark and light times, Car takes Bill and me to another new territory. It needs little time to understand that this is trimming territory again. This time it is a womanperson and she is not too bad. I cannot see it now, but it feels like an improvement when she has done with me.

When we are back home, I can see that Marjolyn and Bill like it a lot. Can you really understand that?

Well, okay folks if you are happy, I am happy too. It still isn't my favorite pastime and not even ten cookies are enough compensation.

I think.

When Charley is being trimmed, Joy joins him.

The apple and the ball

It is a nice, warm and sunny day and we are mostly in the outside territory. I even get my food outside, after we have been to the woods.

My drink is there as well and I have my soft place to lie on. I am not so active, because of the heat. The Joy-Cat joins me. She feels also quite hot, as far as I can see, because she stretches and makes herself very long and remains in that stretched position. I imitate her and when I stretch my hind paws it is nice and cool, because my belly is on the stones. Really cool.

It is a differentday. In our territory there are many days that Bill and Marjolyn are in their everydayplace, but sometimes there are days that they change their habits. Those are the days when Marjolyn also comes to the woods and we do everything together.

So today is a differentday.

When the differentday is almost ending, Marjolyn takes me to the grass. The grass is a place in our outside territory, where I am not allowed to go by myself and certainly not to pee. That would make my persons very angry.

Anyhow, we are going to the grass and I am given a treat. I can smell it. I can eat it. It looks like a ball and it rolls on the grass. For sure I follow it immediately. I chew on it and that's really something. I can eat this very fast, because the taste is great. In no time the ball has disappeared. Okay that was the ball. Marjolyn gives me another ball. This one is not to be eaten.

It smells okay, but that's it. I chew on it anyhow and the ball squeaks and makes a lot of noise. Also something I like. So I do my very best to keep it squeaking. It takes time to make it stop, which it does quite suddenly. I have chewed too much so that it is fed up with the squeaking. Let's eat it then. Not allowed. Marjolyn takes the ball away and it goes straight into the throwawaythingsbox.

Good-bye ball.

Charley and his ball. The ball that went into the throwawaythingsbox.

The contest

On a morning when I wake up, I can feel that something special is going to happen today. Yesterday a lot of time has been spent in combing and trimming and it never stopped. This mostly happens when we get visitors and indeed Karen arrives. I like that very much and I jump up to her as high as I can to say hello.

Better still, Karen also joins us in Car and my House and my dish are coming too. I am even more pleased when I see a big bag of cookies coming along as well.

When Car stops growling, we have arrived in a territory that I don't like at all. It is the trimming territory, where I have been before. There we go again. Is Karen also going to trim me? There is a manperson in the territory and he has a white coat. He touches me everywhere and looks into my mouth. What is this supposed to mean?

My House has come into the territory as well and Marjolyn shows me in. There are many dogs like me and they all have brought their own houses with them.

I have no objection. From my House I can have a good look and survey the whole territory. I am safe. Fortunately there is no trimming going on.

All the persons are sitting in the territory and one manperson is going to talk with a lot of words.

I am rather curious to know what is the issue. One by one the dogs are put on a table. They are not being trimmed, but they are being looked over by a manperson and again this manperson looks in their mouths as well as making a thorough investigation of all their parts. Even in the inside of their ears.

One by one, and accompanied by their manpersons or womanpersons the dogs have to go to the middle of the territory and they have to walk a couple of rounds. When they have finished all the other persons make noises with their paws.

O dear, it seems to be my turn now. I am taken out of my House and Marjolyn and Bill stay seated. Karen comes with me. She puts my leash on and I have to walk some rounds. Only Karen and me in the middle of the territory. They all look at me and I can tell you that I feel rather embarrassed. I think I am going to create a distraction and jump up and down a couple of times. I hope the, like that as well.

Big mistake, because Karen immediately says: Shame! And I have to behave normally and walk properly. Fortunately we finish quickly and I am back in my House. With a cookie, of course. At least that's something positive.

It takes quite some time before I am taken out of my House again and Karen takes me back to the middle of the territory. I have to sit and some manperson puts a dish in front of me. It is shiny but very small. That's not such a good dish for food, because it cannot but contain a very small quantity. Moreover there is no food at all in this dish, not even the smallest cookie. Karen takes the dish to Marjolyn and she says: "Good boy, good boy, Charley"!

Charley and Karen and the shiny dish

The dish is coming back with us. Fortunately I have never had to eat my food out of it. The dish is in the everydayplace of Marjolyn. I don't mind because I don't like it. Too shiny. And much too small for my food.

A birthday party

Marjolyn and Bill have left with Car and they did not take me along. I am now by myself in the small territory and I am in my House. I just wait for them to return and most of the times, they bring many new things into our territory. Food or other things. When the door is opened I always jump up to have a good look at the things that are arriving into our territory.

I can see it immediately if there is something for me. Food or cookies or toys.

The thing they use to make my small territory is not there at the moment and the door is closed, so no way I can see what is happening on the other side. I jump against the door to see if I can open it, but no way.

On the other side I can hear the Joy-Cat. She jumps against the door as well. The thing persons use to open the door is quite high, but the Joy-Cat can also jump very high and I have seen before that she is able to open a door. Very exiting, because maybe she is going to open this door as well.

And indeed she does it. The door is open and the Joy-Cat comes in.

Of course, I am going to have a look immediately what's behind the door. When I am alone, I am never allowed into the larger territory. So I take the opportunity to have a good look. Nobody else is there, but the Joy-Cat and me.

I walk around a little in the sitting area of the persons and I can jump on their sitting place.

From there I have a nice view into the outside territory. There isn't much to be seen and it is getting dark.

I jump back on the ground and than I see something strange. It is thin and it lies in a coil. It looks like something in the woods, but not too much. It is quite long and attached to the lightmaker in the territory. Bill and Marjolyn always use the lightmaker when the dark comes.

I have to investigate this and the best way is always to chew on it.

I continue my endeavors until the coil is broken. I still don't know what it is, but it didn't taste nice either.

The outside territory is dark and the inside territory as well. When Bill and Marjolyn are there and it is dark, they always make light in the inside territory. But since they are not there now, the dark stays.

Car is returning and that's why I know that Bill and Marjolyn are coming back. I am gong to say hello to them, because they like that very much and moreover I have to have a close look at the incoming goods.

There are many new things and I am given a very large cookie. Great thing and I take it to my House.

Marjolyn enters the large territory and she makes a lot of noise. I think something is very wrong.

Bill joins her and they are walking up and down in the sitting area. Marjolyn points out the coil, which I have been chewing on and it is many times shame again. A piece of the coil is stuck in the ground and Bill takes it out. He takes the coil and the lightmaker from the sitting area to some place else.

He fixes the pieces of the coil together.

Finally the lightmaker goes back to the sitting area and Marjolyn makes the light in the territory.

We all sit down in the sitting area and there are drinks and treats. Marjolyn is making nice noises and even Bill joins in.

They look at me and when they have finished their noise, they both pick me up and hug me. When I am back on the ground, I look the other way. I think my persons are behaving rather funny. It must have something to do with the coil, but I am not totally sure about it.

The stick

I have learnt a new word. The word is Stick. Stick is nice, because Stick is a toy in the woods. When I didn't 't yet know what Stick was supposed to be, I have left many of them lying around on the ground. They were just things available on the ground of the woods and they didn't 't smell like anything nice. It is something from the trees.

One day Bill picked it up from the ground and he threw it away. I had no idea why he did that, so I ran after it to investigate. He had touched it so his smell was on it. That made the thing ours, so to speak. So what do you do as a good doggy? You pick it up and bring it to Bill. I stand in front of him and he wants to grasp the thing. Since I was the one to get it, I don't really like it too much to give it back to him immediately.

Besides that I think that a good chew should give me an idea about its ed'bility. I taste it well and thoroughly, but must come to the conclusion that it is nothing more than rubbish.

Nevertheless I continue to chew until there is hardly anything left. When I start on a job I like to finish it properly.

Well, you might think that was it then, but no nothing is less true, because Bill picks up another thing from the ground and talks to me about it. Okay, let's pay attention, because the word he says isn't exactly known to me.

"Charley, watch me", says Bill and as you remember this means that I have to look at him. I look up at him to listen to what comes next. "Stick, Stick, Charley, Stick" says Bill again and immediately he throws the thing high into the air. It drops down in the middle of the bushes.

I am after it at my fastest, of course. I sniff and sniff and vaguely I can smell Bill's smell. I ferret it out and pick it up. But not fast enough since Bill is calling me again and this time it's "Come".

I keep the thing in my mouth and run to Bill and drop down in front of him so that I can start my chewing activities. This thing is a lot tougher than the previous one and it is big business to break it into pieces. Bill grasps the thing at the other end and we both pull at the same time. This time I let him win, just to see what happens now.

That doesn't take much time because Bill says "Stick" again and he shows me the thing. In the past few weeks I have understood that persons have a word for every item, so I listen carefully to get this word.

Between you and me, I must say that dogs have a great advantage, because everything I can see or smell, is immediately known to me and I always know quite well whether it 's food or not. So frankly speaking I don't need all those words.

Well, what can I say: a thing that drops from a tree and stays on the ground, which is not food, but can be chewed on, is Stick.

In the meantime Bill has thrown Stick quite far away and I am going to find Stick for him. Practically speaking you can play the same game with Stick as with Ball.

Again something to remember carefully.

We return back home and as soon as my hairs are completely dry, I am allowed in the larger territory. Since I no longer have "little accidents" in our territory – you know what I mean – I am allowed more and more often in the larger territory.

I look around and I realize that there are many Sticks in this territory. These Sticks are part of the chairs where the persons can sit on (and me too from time to time).

They are fixed to the chairs so it 's impossible to throw them away, but I don 't mind that very much, because it still remains possible to chew on these sticks. So let's go to work on it.

That particular afternoon I have understood that there is a considerable difference between the Sticks in the woods and the Sticks in the territory. I shall not repeat what I have had to listen to. Many words that I had not heard until that time and all spoken with the darkest of voices. Not one of my best moments.

Charley and Cooper

One day all my things are disappearing into Car and we are going to sit in Car as well. When Car stops growling, I can see it immediately, we are in the territory of Karen and Hans.

Aha, this will be fun, because there is also a dog in their territory. We both leave for the outside territory to play together.

My House is standing next to his soft place. I have inspected this soft place, but I prefer my House (by the way, he doesn't 't seem to have a House) and also my other things. My food and cookies are hidden and I don 't regret that, because although this new dog is a nice guy and he loves to play, I cannot have it that he would have a go at my food and my cookies.

Karen puts my leash on and I go outside with her. Bill and Marjolyn are leaving with Car. I stay with Karen and the other dog.

It is a nice place to be and I am not making a fool of myself and I will not think about Bill and Marjolyn. They will certainly be back to pick me up again.

There are many light and dark times and in the meantime I learn that the other dog is called Cooper and Cooper has very dark hairs.

Cooper and I play a lot together and we have had many runs in the woods that are close to Karen's territory. Sometimes we also met another dog. That dog is called Spots. And I know why; his hairs are light but he has many small dark spots.

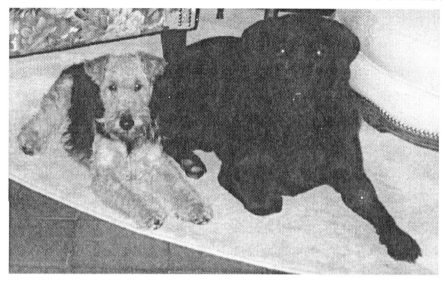

Charley and Cooper

One day I am running up and down in the inside territory. Karen is also running up and down and we bump into each other. She drops on the ground and makes a lot of noise. It is not a good noise and I can feel that she is hurting.

Hans and Karen disappear with their shiny beast and when they return, Karen has something around her paw. I think it is because she hurts.

When the new day comes, another shiny beast is arriving, and a manperson that I know well is coming out of it. It is one of the manpersons who is called Jack. He often comes to the territory where I live with Marjolyn and Bill.

He puts my House and my things into his shiny beast and me too. I wonder what is going to happen now. It is quite strange.

Jack takes me to his own territory. Although it is close to my territory, where I live with Bill and Marjolyn, we are not going home. I don't understand this very well.

It is nice to be with Jack, because he takes me everywhere. I am forever sitting in his shiny beast. With him I have seen many new things. Some persons are coming into his territory. Again some persons that I don 't know. They are very friendly and I am receiving a lot of food from the persons table.

When it is dark I have to go into my House. But the door has not been closed, so that I can go into the rest of the territory and therefore during the dark I slept on Jack's sitting place. The next day when he found me there, he did not even say that it was a shame. I like Jack. Yes I do. And he has nice cookies too.

After some light and dark times Bill and Marjolyn came to

pick me up. I was quite happy to be back in my own territory

and fortunately the Joy-Cat was there again.

Swimming party

It is a differentday and I am going out with Bill and Marjolyn and Car. It doesn't take long and I am allowed to sit with Marjolyn and I do not need to lie on the ground.

We get out of Car and Bill takes me for a long walk. It is a place that I have never seen before. Not like the woods but a large area with grass and small trees.

In the very distance I can see persons and dogs. So that makes me curious and we walk a little faster.

When we are closer I can see that I know these persons. They are the womanpersons and the dogs of the school. This is great. I am off my leash and all of us are running around and making noises and having fun.

Now, all of a sudden something is happening that I have never seen before. The persons are now almost only in their bare skins and we all walk towards a very large pool of water.

I smell a rat if you understand my meaning, but fortunately I don 't see one. And indeed, my fears come true. Bill and I are going into this pool.

I am getting wetter and wetter and the water is higher and higher. It is getting so high that I cannot even touch the ground with my paws anymore. This gives me the feeling that I have to move my paws very fast, so that I don 't sink into this pool. Bill also takes his paws from the ground and is struggling in the water. We struggle together. It comes to a point that all the persons and the dogs are struggling together.

In my opinion the struggling takes far too much time and I am as glad as I can be when we finally feel the ground again. The persons and the dogs are dried with towels.

Bill puts his cloths on and we walk all the way back. Marjolyn is waiting for us with Car. She did not come to struggle.

I think she is a very smart person, because struggling is no good. I prefer to walk in my woods.

Cleaning

Some things and some days in our inside territory, I don't like at all. Such as days of much noise and a womanperson, who is continuously walking up and down. In the beginning I had no idea what was going to happen, but after many light and dark times and the same womanperson I know the issue. Cleaning is going on. There is this shiny beast, a very very small one, which crawls on the ground and makes a lot of noise. It is a very dangerous beast. It doesn't have a head, but it does have a snout and a long neck and one day not so long ago I saw this snout gobbling up something that it had found on the ground. Immediately I ran to my House. That was bad luck, because my soft place had gone. Apparently it also had to be cleaned.

Well, I can tell you, for me this cleaning business is nonsense.

So I went back to the sitting place in Bill's everydayplace. For a long time no problem and the noise stopped. When that's the case what can you do but being an interested Welsh terrier? You are going back to have a look. Clever enough, because at this moment the womanperson was walking around with a long stick, which has many long hairs, attached to it, so that at first I thought it was an animal. I didn't like that animal at all and made the immediate decision to attack. I had the impression that the womanperson participated in the attack, because she moved the stick up and down very quickly. Fortunately I saw in time that the animal was unreal, but nevertheless I attacked this animal many times afterwards, whenever I saw him around, but I admit that the results have been poor.

Whenever the womanperson goes away the unreal animal and the small shiny beast disappear into the dark area, somewhere in our territory.

This womanperson, who is coming to clean our house, (I still cannot understand why) is very friendly to me and sometimes when Bill and Marjolyn are not at home, she takes me out for a walk. I try to make her understand that she has to let me go by myself when we are in the woods, but until now I have not been successful.

A very nice moment is the time that she sits down in the area where we have our makefoodplace, and sits to have food and drink. I always get my cookie from her and that is a great compensation for all this cleaning activity.

There is also a manperson, who belongs to the womanperson of the cleaning. He is also a friendly person and he takes me out for a walk from time to time. Regretfully also he doesn't seem to understand that I can walk by myself when we are in the woods.

Well, never mind, these persons do not speak my language and they can only understand something when they use their own words. I don't need words, but would not mind to be able to use them from time to time.

The dishes

In our makefoodplace we have many boxes to contain the foodstuffs that Marjolyn and Bill are always using. They have dishes and all kind of other things they need to prepare their food and also little boxes and sticks and packages. The whole place is full of things that are necessary for the preparation of our food. I know exactly which cupboard contains my own food. I cannot reach it and up till now I have not been successful to open it, but it is enough to see Bill or Marjolyn approach this cupboard. At that moment I know that something very nice is going to happen.

When they are busy in this way, I am always present and sit or lie close to them to survey the happenings. I always want to know the proceedings.

When they have had their food, they never clean their dishes with their tongues, like I do. Those dishes and other things are put into a water box.

But before that happens, I always help with the cleaning.

Charley helps doing the dishes

It is a shame that all kind of little bits of the food is still on those dishes and has not been eaten at all. Such a thing would never happen to me. I always eat everything I have in my dish till the very last crumb.

Incredibly enough, I am not allowed to help with the cleaning, because you can count on it, every time that I start to do this finishing job, Bill or Marjolyn immediately lock the door of the water box.

I don't know whether other dogs have these same problems.

Snow

One day when I wake up, there is light, but it is different from the normal light. It makes me quite curious.

Bill is coming to get me and we go outdoors immediately.

When the door is open, I stand still. Our outside territory has gone, the street has gone, and the grass has gone. The sounds are quite different.

Everything has been covered with white and cold and it sticks to my paws when I walk on it. The sounds are muffled.

We walk the way to the woods, but I cannot detect any known smell.

I would not know where to pee to make known that I was there.

Have my friends been here before me? I cannot smell them at all. Not even Rascal and as you know I am very keen on him. There is nothing else but to raise my paw somewhere in the middle of nowhere; so that the others may know that I have been there before them.

Charley in the snow

Also in the woods everything is quite different. I have to stop many times, just to see what it is all about.

By the way, the white is quite cold and I can feel it with my paws. So it is the best solution not to stand still for more than a very short moment. Wow, something is happening now. Bill grasps the white stuff with his paws and makes a ball out of it. He throws the ball far away. That means that I have to run to get it.

Forget it, because the moment I have the ball in my mouth, is has disappeared. Only a very little bit of white stuff of the ball remains on the ground.

For a couple of light and dark times the white is there and then one day everything is back to normal. The white has gone.

Will it be back some day?

The pet hotel

Again there is such a day that many unusual things are happening. Quite different from the normal things. I can always feel that and so I stay in the neighborhood of Bill and Marjolyn, because then at least I can see immediately what they are doing. They are busy walking up and down with all kind of things and that is all I can say for the moment.

I can see that the Joy-Cat is put inside her house and she is not happy with it, because she starts making a lot of loud catnoises. A box of food is coming with us and then we all go inside Car, but my House isn't there with us this time. We do not have to drive a long distance to arrive in a new territory. It smells like many animals.

We enter the territory and a manperson approaches us. He puts me on a leash, not my own, and I have to go with him. The Joy-Cat is still in her house making a lot of noise.

The new manperson takes me to an outside territory. He lets me go and normally speaking I would like that, but at this moment it is meaningless to me. It is no fun in that territory. There is another dog, a womandog. Well, at least that is something. I walk up and down a little bit and can hear the growling of Car. He goes away. I cannot see Bill and Marjolyn. I go to the door and try to pry it open with my paws. I am not successful. I stay there in hopes that one of my persons is coming for me.

They are not, but the manperson who took me there is coming to get me. On the leash again and we walk to a new and very small territory. The womandog is also coming along. Together we are locked in that territory. There is a soft place but it is not my own and I am not at ease at all, but what can you do but lie down on it. It takes a very long time and I am not ashamed to say that I am crying a little (only a little, but still). I want to be with my own persons and in my own territory and in my own House.

The new manperson brings some food. Well at least that is something. The Joy-Cat has totally disappeared and I cannot even hear her any longer. Will she be someplace else with another cat?

There are no cookies in this territory and nobody plays with a ball or a stick. My Letgo is not with me as well, but maybe that is for the best, because there could always be a chance that the womandog takes it from me.

There are many light and dark times and then suddenly the manperson takes me along on the leash. We go in another direction and not to the usual outdoor place. I hear Bill's voice and I am very very happy. I jump higher than ever. Car is there as well and the Joy-Cat in her house. She is again making a lot of her catnoise. It is only a short trip, but all the time that we are inside Car I continue to jump up and down. I want Bill to understand that I am very very happy.

In our territory all is well and the same as usual. The smell is wonderful and my House is there again and my own soft place.

I get a cookie.

My own swimming pool

It is a warm day and we are all in the outdoor territory. When the day is almost over, persons are coming to visit and they also sit in t e outdoor territory. There is food and drink, but I do not get anything. It is just for the persons. There is also a very small person who runs around a lot, but whenever I want to play with him, he runs away with much noise.

I think he is scared of me. Very silly, because the only thing I am interested in is to play.

The big persons and the small person are going to play on the grass with a ball. Yes, you understand me correctly, a ball. I am not allowed to come along. I cannot even go there, because the grass territory is closed off. I can just look. This is the baddest luck ever. Not my day today.

Well, you never can tell. I am going to try if I can join them all the same.

My best chance is the low gate between the water of the ponds. Slowly slowly one paw after the other I try. It is really very difficult.

How it happened I do not know, but suddenly I am in the water. My head and everything went under. I started to struggle immediately, because I remembered the struggling from the day that I went to the pool with Bill. I try to get out, because like the other time I am not exactly amused. Marjolyn is running towards me, and she

Charley inspects his pool

pulls me out of the water. She makes a lot of noise. I have a feeling that she likes it.

Of course, I am being dried and put back in the outside territory.

The game with the ball goes on and again I play no role in it.

Then suddenly something happens. The ball is thrown into my direction, but it drops into the water. This is an irresistible situation; I cannot let go and have to take my chance. I jump into the water and go straight for the ball. The struggling after all is not a problem and I get hold of the ball easily.

And if you think that the persons like it? No, not at all! Again I am taken out of the water. I have to give up the ball. I am thoroughly dried with a towel.

Struggling isn't too bad if you have a purpose, but certainly I prefer to stay on the ground if I am not given the ball after all.

Bowie

On a differentday a manperson is coming to visit and he is not alone. No, he has a big dog that belongs to him. That could be fun, because this means walking together in the woods.

Indeed, me, Bill and Marjolyn and the manperson and his dog are going to the woods. It is a mandog like me.

When we are walking by ourselves in the woods, I run with him for a short while, but this mandog keeps looking for his manperson and doesn't even look at me. Playing, no way.

Okay, than I shall have to make my rounds by myself.

I find him a bit sad and that's why I offer him my ball. I shall never do that again, because gone is my ball. In his big mouth and until the moment that we reach our territory it is absolutely impossible to get it back.

I could fix my gaze on Bill till dark times, but he didn't seem to understand or didn't want to understand, because he took no action to give my ball back to me.

The new manperson and his dog, which had to put all his paws in a dish with water before he was allowed inside our territory, stay for a long time.

Joy-Cat comes to have a look at this new dog, but he doesn't even look at her, so that she just walks away to her soft place, with her tail straight up and her head upright, like she does when she is disagreeable about something.

We are given some cookies, so that's something, but more than staying down this dog is not doing. I stretched out as well and have taken the opportunity to have a good look at him.

Well, I can tell you that he looks a lot different from me. To start with, he is divided in two parts. His front part with his paws is in a light color, whereas his back part and his paws are made of a dark color. In my opinion he cannot see much, because the hairs on his head are totally covering his eyes. For that reason I cannot see his eyes and I don't like that at all.

Charley and Bowie

At a certain moment the new manperson is leaving and the dog is not going with him.

Well have you ever; this one is going to stay. His things are brought into our territory and a big box with his soft place and a dish for his food, but he doesn't seem to have any food with him. Does he get my food?

I have to pay careful attention that all my cookies will not disappear in this big mouth. I must be alert.

After some dark and light times I understand that his name is Bowie.

He still doesn't talk to me and keeps to himself. Joy-Cat has given up and doesn't look at him any more.

All in all Bowie is quite modest, because he never touches my dish and food or my things or my cookies, but I have to be careful with my ball, because if he happens to pick it up, he never gives it back. So I take care that he cannot take it from me, but that's hard work and none too easy.

By the way, growling doesn't help at all, because he doesn't seem to hear me.

On a certain day in the woods he is walking slightly ahead of us, and an old dog is approaching us. I know him and I have always tried to avoid him, because he is not very friendly. A lot of growling means that it is best to keep your distance.

Bowie doesn't hear it and I can see it happen. This is not going to work out well. The old one is going to attack Bowie. I admit that I do not think Bowie exactly my sort of friend, but nevertheless I cannot accept to have a dog of my group attacked by a stranger.

Let's get at it and see to it that the old one is taken out of combat. It has served another purpose as well, because Bowie now knows who is in charge in our group.

Isn't it?

Since that time Bowie is friendlier, but I continue to be on the alert.

Many Welsh Terriers

We are in for another day with Car and this time Bowie is going to join us. He has to stay in the back part of Car and I am with Marjolyn.

Well, where are we going today? I am curious. My things are coming with us as well.

When Car stops growling, we are in the middle of the woods. Not ours but another one. I am having my dish and food right there. I can only hope that nobody is passing, because you never know what happens then. I prefer to have my meals at home.

We all walk to another area and we can see a lot of persons and to my surprise many dogs like myself. I feel a bit ashamed about Bowie with his long hairs and his invisible eyes, because he sticks out between all these Welshes. Certainly everybody can see that.

Anyhow, fortunately nobody seems to care about it. There is food and drink for the persons and when they have finished, a manperson is going to talk. Well we have to see what is happening. I have quite a good feeling about it.

After a while we are starting to walk. The whole group is going into the same direction into these woods. And Bowie is coming along as well.

There are many puddles in the woods and I try to avoid them as much as I can. Incredibly, there are many Welshes who walk right through these puddles and they look very dirty. I don't even want to think about it, because I know exactly how this is going to end if I would do that. Much drying activity with the towel and to stay in the small territory when we are back home.

To walk in these woods is only half fun, because nobody is running free. All of us are on the leashes. Our speed is moderate.

After a while all the persons and dogs stop walking. Some of the persons have flashes and they flash around quite a lot. Bill is also flashing and believe it or not Bowie is not allowed to join the Welsh group. He has to wait all by himself in a separate place. I feel a bit sorry for him, because now everybody can see that he is different.

We return to the place where we started and in the meantime there are many new things to be seen. Aha, this is great. Now I can really show all my tricks.

Just imagine there are cookies suspended from the tree, which you can only get if you jump very high. That's my type of business and I jump like an idiot to get at the cookies.

No big deal and I grab one after the other. My mouth is full of cookies and, of course, that means trouble with Bill. I cannot but save one single cookie.

In another place there is a long dark bag. No problem, I remember this bag from the school.

The group of Welshes

For me this is peanuts. I enter the bag easily. There are many more tricks to be performed. Crouch low to pass under a tree. I refuse to do this. What nonsense is this? I jump over it. My specialty is jumping, you know.

One thing I absolutely refused to do, to sit in a rolling box and to be carried around by a person. The Welshes who did that looked very unhappy. So when they put me into this rolling box, I jumped out of it immediately.

This was really too much.

All together I found this a very pleasant day and after all they gave me all those cookies I had grabbed from the tree. And that's just as it should be.

Not so good Charley

Bowie has been staying in our territory for many dark and light times now and in the beginning he was very quiet and modest and he seemed to understand that I am calling the shots here. But actually this is changeing a bit and I get this feeling that he would like to be boss as well.

It always starts with my ball in the woods. Once he has grabbed it, there is no way to get it back.

Okay, let's play with a stick then. But that doesn't help, because wherever I go, he goes too.

I start to be fairly annoyed, but how to make him understand. I cannot look at him and show him by meaningful looks what I want and besides that he doesn't seem to hear me.

I have to think about it carefully, because there is always this great danger that he starts to boss me around and that is something I do not even want to consider for one minute.

On a certain day he went away with Bill and Car. I was very curious to know whereto and I didn't like it at all that I could not come along as well.

But how many laughs I had when he came back. All his long hairs had disappeared and his hair was trimmed as short as mine can be. I thought that it was a good thing that finally such a disaster happened to him as well, because until now, I was the only one for the trimming.

Okay, he had lost a lot of hairs and looked quite different from his normal looks. Certainly it was an advantage that his eyes were visible now.

I made good use of that the next day in the woods. He went to the stick that had been thrown for me and I looked at him with an expression of severity in my eyes to make him understand that the stick was mine. It stands to reason that I use my growling voice at the same time, but that is not something that works with him.

Well, the meaningful looking didn't help either, because he just went for my stick.

This time I was just able to manage to get there before him, but his bossy behavior was not pleasing me at all.

One time when it was dark, we had made our last rounds of the day. When we return our food is always ready and after that it's bedtime.

I have my food in my usual place and he has his in another place that I cannot reach. When we have finished our dishes are taken away.

This time while I go for my House and bed I pass his eating-place and what do I see his dish is still there. I go for it immediately, because this is a great moment to show him who is the boss in this territory.

That went very wrong, because while I grabbed him by his head, he grabbed me in one of my paws. So my action was quite useless.

I am truly ashamed about what happened.

I almost don't dare to have it written down, but it was really only meant to show that I am the boss.

Bill and Marjolyn came running fast and I was picked up at my hind paws and pulled high into the air. Dreadful. I was absolutely powerless.

Bill and Marjolyn were very unfriendly to me and they have not understood at all that my only purpose was to show Bowie a lesson. I have not had a cookie in my House that evening and my head hurt badly.

Besides that it hasn't served as a lesson after all, because he still looking at my food and my cookies and there is no respect for my ball or my stick.

From time to time we had our difference of opinion and therefore we have never become great friends.

He is gone now. He was ill on a certain moment and he wasn't very active any more. Bill took him along with Car one day and Bill came back alone and I have never seen Bowie again.

Find

There is a game in the woods that is very difficult and frankly speaking I don't always understand quite well what Bill means with it.

H e throws a stick or a ball. That's easy to follow.

With this new game, the stick or the ball is in a place that I cannot see. Bill says a word and this word is "Find"! And after that he says: " Ball" or "Stick".

The first few times I didn't see a ball or a stick, so I stood just there to see if I could discover the ball somehow. Nothing. Bill said again and again: "Charley, Find, Find". But the ball didn't show up and he went to get it himself. I didn't see the fun of this game at all.

Bill played this game many, many times and finally when the day came that I understood what Let go meant, it was also the day that I understood about Find.

Well, it is just like this, Letgo is somewhere in our territory and then Bill says: "Charley, find Letgo". I f I hear the word for

Letgo, I want to look for Letgo immediately and I search him everywhere. Of course, I can find him and I take him to Bill immediately. This means: "Good boy, good boy".

This is the way we now play this game in the woods with the ball and if I cannot see the ball I have to find him, just as with Letgo.

Sometimes it isn't easy and then Bill comes to help me.

A new trimming place

Today the dark has come when we go out with Car. I am alone with Bill and it doesn't take long before Car stops growling again.

Aha, I can come along, because my leash is put on.

We arrive in a new territory, where I can smell a couple of dogs. I can also hear them, because when we enter the territory they all start barking.

A new manperson is in the territory and I feel that I have seen him before. I don't know exactly but I think it had to do with the day of all the Welshes and I got many cookies from the tree.

Let's see what is going to happen. Bill and the new manperson take me inside. The other dogs aren't there, but I can smell them very well.

I am just thinking a bit what all this means and I am put down on a table by this new manperson.

Bill is leaving. He dares to leave me here all alone. I don't like it at all. This is not my idea of fun.

Besides that I discover that the new manperson has put me on a, o no this cannot be true, trimming table. I am carefully tied with some leashes and unable to move anywhere.

I just close my eyes and let it happen. I wouldn't know anyhow what else to do. It takes a long time, but I have to admit, it isn't half as bad as the other trimming occasions.

I see many of beautiful hairs disappear. I shall be quite cold later on.

Finally the trimming is ready and I am just waiting. I would love to have a cookie now, but they are not being distributed in this territory. Then it is better to be at the pet doctor's, who sometimes gives a cookie away.

The door is opened and Marjolyn comes in. I am being picked up and my persons haven't forgotten me, because that's always the question. They just leave you somewhere and you never know whether they come back or not. At home I don't mind, because then I am in my own territory, but when you are in a strange territory you never know. No I am not for it.

Marjolyn and the manperson are talking together. It's about me I can feel it, because my knowledge of the human language is getter better and better. The word nice means that my trimming has been successful. And certainly I like to hear that. I shall try to find out tomorrow if I totally agree.

Back home in our territory, fortunately there are some cookies.

Since that time I have returned many times to the same manperson for my trimming.

It remains a nasty business, but I don't feel too bad in his territory. By the way some time ago I saw the same manperson somewhere else and just for a short moment I was quite scared that he would start trimming me. Fortunately there were no trimming table, but just tables for the persons to eat from. The manpersons and the womanperson, who belongs to him, had three dogs and they are almost like Welshes. At least I had seen them, because it remains a strange thing that whenever I go to their territory to be trimmed, I never see them.

They were quite friendly, but they were not allowed to run by themselves, so there wasn't much playing.

This happened the day that we went somewhere outside close to very disgusting water, but that story will be told another time.

The bath

Sometimes Marjolyn goes to a place in our territory where she can sit in a big box, which is filled with water. It is like a pool but much smaller. She cannot struggle in this box, but all the same there is a lot of water. Sometimes I join her just to have a look. The water doesn't smell nice and I have to cough if I sniff at it.

She is totally in the water in this box and she seems to like it.

Sometimes I lie down on a soft place in front of the box, and I wait for her to get out of it. I don't take the risk to look over the rim anymore, because in the beginning when I did that (I really have to know and investigate everything) Marjolyn made a big ball from the stuff in the waterbox and she put it on my head.

This ball was very soft and rolled just from my head on the ground. I thought, "Get it" but that was a big mistake. It tasted absolutely awful. I never want to try that again.

Charley takes a bath

Another day there was a small manperson in our territory.
He stayed many light and dark times and he slept on the soft
place in Marjolyn's everydayplace. The small manperson also
went in to the waterbox and he also sat in the white stuff.

The small manperson made a lot of noise and I found that
quite interesting. So I went the re to see him. Again a mistake,
because he also made a ball of the white stuff and stupid me,

grab it again, because after all I am a good sport. It was as distasteful as the first time.

When the small manperson was dried with a towel, he put the towel over my head. I wasn't wet at all, because I didn't go into this waterbox, but nevertheless the towel.

As I said I like to be a good sport and to participate is the best solution. So I accepted this silly towel game. I even walked around with the towel over my head. That was something the small manperson liked a lot, because he made loud noises and I could see his teeth. Since some time I know the word to express the meaning of this, it is laugh.

From time to time I also show my teeth. It is not always to show that I am angry, but instead to show that I have fun too and I put my mouth wide open.

Is that laughing you think?

And Car again....

On a day with nice weather, I can see it happen. This is to be a day that we go out with Car again. My dish is coming along, my cookies and a towel. I follow it closely. My House and Letgo are not coming. They have to stay in our territory and the Joy-Cat stays there as well. She always stays in the territory an never comes along on our trips with Car.

Now I have to wait and see where we are going. I am on the ground at Bill's feet. Marjolyn makes that Car does what she want him to do. It is a long distance. From time to time I get up to try and see if there is something interesting outside. There are all kind of places I don't know at all. Nothing from my street or my woods.

Car stops growling now and I jump up. Where are we? My leash is put on. That is a good sign, because it means that we are going out of Car. Bill takes me for a walk and I can raise my leg thoroughly. Very good, I had some needs after this long trip.

The back of Car is opened up and my dish and my food are coming out of it. I get my meal in this strange place. I don't like it too much because I have to pay careful attention to see if nobody approaches us who could get at my food. The drink is also coming out of Car.

When everything is finished, Car is closed and we start walking. It is a sort of woods and there are some hairy animals that I have never seen before. They eat from the grass. Something I am not allowed to do. They don't make noises. They look at me. but a little bit of nice nosing is out of the question.

We are going to an inside territory and a manperson is approaching us. It smells good in this place. According to me this is a good food place with nice things. Marjolyn and Bill are sitting down at a table. I stay on my leash, but sit next to the table and close to Marjolyn and Bill.

There are many more tables in this territory, but no other persons. They arrive a little bit later. Marjolyn tells me to behave and not to make noise, so I just stay there. I try not to look at the persons.

I would love to approach them.

The manperson, who belongs in the territory, brings drinks for my persons and when he comes back again, the dishes for Marjolyn and Bill are put on the table as well.

It smells great and I certainly would love to taste it, but I know perfectly well that there is no chance at all.

They are eating for a long time and from time to time I get up to have a good look at what they are doing.

Suddenly I hear a noise. It is a noise made by the hairy animals outside. It is quite different from anything I have heard before, so I really have to react. Just a small bark.

Like I thought this is instant shame on me and stay where you are. To hold to your own as a Welsh is not always easy. Can nobody understand that I absolutely have to react to such a strange noise? Unthinkable not to respond when you are being talked to.

When Bill says something to Marjolyn, she always talks back immediately.

I am happy again when the manperson from the territory is back. He brings me a dish of water and also a small dish with some food from the persons' table. It is delicious. I polish it off until the last crumb. I drink a bit from the water and after all come to the conclusion that today is one of the good days.

We leave this territory of the tables with the foods and go back to Car. It doesn't take long to arrive at a new territory.

This is fun, because when we are leaving Car, there are some small and big persons and the small persons want to play with me. I run with them in their inside and outside territory, until the water drops from the sky and we can only stay in the inside territory.

There is some more good food for the persons' table, but not for me.

I get a cookie, but they taste like my own cookies, so no news at all.

When the food and drink and the talking by the persons has finished, we go back to Car.

It is a long time in Car and I am going to sleep, because I have had many new experiences today.

Anyhow I am always glad to be back in my own territory. The Joy-Cat was happy too, because she came to say hello to us immediately.

Tennis

In our woods there are some places where I am not allowed to come. These places are open territories and they have a hard surface, like in our inside territory.

In these places the persons many times play with balls.

In the beginning I thought that I could join them for this game.

These persons play with a ball in a different way than I do. They don't take the ball in their mouth, but they have something in their paws that they use to throw the ball to other persons. From one to the other. Quite funny, but sincerely I prefer to do this with my mouth. For me it is a lot easier to grab the ball that way. These persons with those things loose the balls many times and so I saw my chance at a certain moment to try and join them for the ball game.

The ball came right into my direction and I went for it. Frankly speaking I heard Bill call me and he spoke the Come word, but I wanted to grab that ball so much that I just was not able to follow his command.

I know very well that shame is on me then, but I could not do it. I really couldn't.

So the ball was mine and the persons of the ball seemed to like it, because they made much noise and they came towards me. I waited for them with the ball to see whether we could start our games. And of course when the persons approach me I step back a little bit. ,because certainly the ball remains with me. When they were very close I could see after all that they were angry and regretfully Bill was angry as well. I put in a lot of work and effort to try and keep the ball, but in the end I had to let it go. It was too much shame on me.

Nowadays when we pass that territory, my leash is attached, so that I cannot go there.

That's a pity because I still would love to play ball with these persons.

Or can it possibly be that they don't like it?

Football

In my woods there are other places where persons play with balls. These persons play with a very large ball. A ball that I absolutely cannot take in my mouth.

The small persons that play with it don't take the ball in their mouth but they move the ball with their paws.

They play with this ball in a large open territory. Whenever we pass close to this territory I am immediately in the field.

I have to confess that it is quite heavy, because I cannot take this ball in my mouth, as I said, so also for me it is work of paws. But since I can use all my paws to run and am better equipped than the persons, it is not too difficult after all.

The small persons normally speaking like it when I start playing with them, but when the big persons are playing with their ball I am never allowed to participate. Then it is much shame on me again and some time ago there was a big manperson who wanted to kick me with his paw.

It gave me a feeling to want to chew his paw, but you better don't believe that Bill ever allows such an action, so I ran away very fast. These manpersons cannot catch me anyhow.

Nowadays I play the same sort of game with Bill, using a smaller ball and I am quite good at it and can even catch the ball in midair with my mouth.

Would you be able to imitate me?

Tara's house

Today Car takes us somewhere again. I don't know where and it takes quite some time. When Car stops growling and I am getting out, we are in an unknown territory. There is only one persons house and grass and trees.

From the persons' house some persons are coming to meet us. I know them, but it is a long time ago that we met.

And then. Yes then there is Tara and I remember her very well. She is approaching me to say hello, but all the same she is walking around me a bit and keeping a certain distance. Maybe this is because I am in her territory now. Moreover she is not on her leash and so she can get anywhere and I am still on my leash. So no chance to have a look by myself.

We stay outdoors and I discover some of Tara's toys. She just lets me play by myself and I have the feeling that she doesn't like me anymore. So I shall try to get off my leash, so that I can walk around and take a better look. It works and I start running around the house. This house has many nice surprises. Walking flying animals and other animals that are making noises I have never heard before. No dogs certainly, because they are eating grass. There is no animal of the Cat type. Tara's persons give me her toys. I can smell that. Aha, an unreal animal that squeaks. This is too much and I really cannot resist showing the animal that he is no match for me and certainly this animal isn't Charley proof. So he is taken away from me. Bill doesn't allow it.

When the persons have eaten and drunk and Tara and I have had some of Tara's cookies, we all go with Car. Tara is sitting in the back with her persons.

It doesn't take long and we leave Car again. New woods. That's always exiting. Tara and me are liberated from our leashes and we immediately go to inspect to a long stretch of water. It is not too deep, so we are having a close look at it. We walk in the water, which is quite something for me, as you will remember. The persons keep their paws on dry territory.

And then something very strange happens. There are some new persons and a sort of dog belongs to their group as well. Very different from Tara or me it is.

Its persons are calling my name, so I go to say hello to them immediately. This other dog is also running towards his persons. Bill calls me again and then the other dog also runs towards Bill.

My persons and the other dog's persons are talking together and although I cannot precisely follow this conversation, I understand that this other dog is called Charley, just like me. This astonishes me, because I really thought to be the only one called Charley. This means to pay careful attention to follow the right persons. Am I glad that I have an excellent nose to smell this out, because I would not like to make a mistake.

We went back to Tara's house and have had a lot of treats. Tara's Marjolyn gave us many things. Not too bad this visit. I like that.

Letgo

When I was still a young Welsh and quite new in our territory, they gave me something very nice. It was a something to chew on and to bite and that I could use to play with all persons who like playing with me. Bill and I always pull at this thing and you can imagine that I am practically always the strongest and then Bill lets it go and says so. At least that's what I thought. He said, "Let go, let go" and then he no longer held on to this thing.

For this reason I called this thing Letgo.

I have the utmost fun with Letgo, because I can always get him when I like to play with him. He is always waiting for me. Sometimes, however, Letgo disappears and then suddenly there is a new Letgo. This new Letgo is not too much mine, since it doesn't smell very much like me. I have recently discovered what happens. Marjolyn puts my Letgo in the grumblebox that is next to my House and when this box stops grumbling, Letgo and some other things, like my soft place and my towel, are coming out of the box. Letgo is then not really my own Letgo anymore, because he doesn't smell right.

I take care of that by thoroughly thrashing Letgo, so that he becomes mine again.

Marjolyn has solved this problem in a nice way. We have two Letgoes. So I am never without a nice-smelling Letgo.

Now that I am a bit older and understand better what happens in our territory, gradually I started to understand that Letgo isn't called Letgo at all. It gave me a hard time, because I had gotten used to his name, but I absolutely don't want anybody to think that I am stupid, so I accepted the situation that Letgo isn't called Letgo at all.

It is like this, that Letgo is a very awful word. Let go means that you have to let go everything you just conquered and that is really the limit for a real and well equipped Welsh. Practically unacceptable.

I still don't like it at all when the let go word comes and I just try not to listen to it. Only when it is really impossible to ignore it, I shall let go. Yes, yes.

It occurred to me that when Marjolyn and Bill and I were busy with Letgo they used another word. That word is Rope.

And when I had learnt the search word and they always said "Search, Rope", I started to understand that Letgo's name in effect is Rope.

Charley and his Letgo/Rope

I am used to it in the meantime and have a strict rule: when Marjolyn and Bill have finished with their dishes and are still sitting at the table, I immediately go and get Rope. The exiting element of our game is that I stand close to Bill with Rope in my mouth. The basic idea is that we both start pulling at a side of Rope. Just to see who is the strongest.

After a bit of pulling, Bill says "Charley, down" and immediately afterwards I just drop Rope on the ground. Sometimes, however, he uses the Letgo word and I hate that so much that I just drop Rope even before he says it. It is an exiting moment to see if it's me or Bill getting at Rope first, but mostly I let Bill be first. He throws Rope far away and I go get him. We play this game for some time. Until the moment that Bill gets tired, because then he stops throwing and that's the moment I take Rope with me to my soft place and continue chewing on him for some time.

All in all a nice game for Bill and I like it too.

The observation post

I have an area in our territory where I like to be as often as I can. That's a not allowed area, but when nobody can see it, I am there all the same.

This is the sitting place for the persons and when I position myself on this sitting place I can look outside to see what happens on the street.

There are shiny animals like Car or persons and sometimes other dogs that pass by to go to our woods. They all pass our territory.

And, of course from time to time I can see Rascal passing by with his manperson. I bark and bark very loudly, so that he can certainly hear me. He really has to realize that I live here and that he must never come to my territory, unless I allow it.

Charley on his observation post

When there are other persons coming to our territory Bill and Marjolyn often change their cloths. I can see it immediately and I know the issue.

I leave for my observation post to be the first to see if persons are approaching our territory.

But it is not always the case that new persons are coming, because with those other cloths they sometimes leave our territory and that is practically always a situation that I am not allowed to go with them. In the beginning when I had not yet

148

discovered this fact, I went to the door with them to go out as well, but Bill or Marjolyn then says " Charley, home" and something like watch the house.

So when I see the other cloths situation I go to my observation post immediately, because either they will leave without me - and in that case it is better to watch carefully if everything is all right - or I can see if new persons are coming. I am in the best position whatever the situation.

Whenever the new persons are coming, I can give a warning bark. I know exactly which door they will use and to show that I know that they are there I just run up and down between my observation post and this door.

When the persons have entered our territory I jump and jump as high as I can to see whether they have a package and most of the times they have, something with streamers or smelling nicely and I try to take a good look at it.

Many persons, I must say this, visit us and they always have some treat for me. It is always the womanpersons, who have these treats in a bag.

I am very sorry to see persons coming to us without a bag, because that certainly means no treats.

From time to time they come and have flowers in a crackling paper, but what's that to me. I cannot eat flowers.

The thief

I have done many foolish things in my life, but at the same time I have learnt a lot. And if I may say so, I am getting smarter and smarter in my understanding of the person things.

Therefore it becomes quite easy to grab some treats, when the persons don't pay attention. It happens to me from time to time, because I am very alert to keep control whether there are edible things that I can reach.

The other persons that sometimes visit us always leave at a certain moment, even before they have eaten everything. I would never consider doing that, but well you know persons......

That's my chance and I am immediately at it to finish the leftovers. The handicap, which is those very tiny sticks that are in the food sometimes, can be taken out. I do that with my tongue, because I don't like to eat them. Papers that are sometimes covering the treats can also be destroyed easily, because they don't taste nice as well.

It is a pity that the tiny sticks and the papers remain visible on the ground, because this means that Bill and Marjolyn can see immediately that I have finished the leftovers.

Another thing I have discovered is that on the high side in our makefoodplace, the spot where normally speaking my food is prepared, sometimes treats can be found.

I jump and jump and some time ago I got at one of those. This was top sport because that piece of sausage was not that easy to get.

I had the idea that I really deserved to have it and enjoy the eating of it.

Regretfully there was some difficult paper around it and it took me a very long time to get rid of it. Besides that it is a bore that I had to drop the whole thing on the ground, otherwise it was impossible to get the good part out of it.

I was almost ready with the preparations when Marjolyn came after me with a lot of loud noise.

I kept my mouth thoroughly shut, because when I have gotten hold of something I don't let go if I can avoid it. At first

I thought that Marjolyn said: "Charley, dear, dear", but that was wrong. It was a word that sounds like it a lot, but it wasn't the same and it didn't sound good. That's why I gave in and gave up my treat

So am I dear or thief?

Abroad

Something very special is going to happen. My House and my things are going in Car and also many things that belong to Bill and Marjolyn.

As usual we stay in Car for a long time, but I go down to sleep on a soft place close to Bill's paws.

Car stops growling and I get up to see what is going on. Only Marjolyn gets out and she is doing something with Car. I think he gets his food, because I can hear him gulp.

We go on and I continue my sleep.

When Car stops again, we all get out and I get something to drink from my own dish. Just on the street and as you know, I don't like that very much, but I was quite thirsty. There is a cookie as well. Good enough.

We are going to a person food place. Marjolyn and Bill are getting something to eat. When they have finished their dishes, we get back to Car and Bill takes me for an extra walk, so that I can takes care of my needs. It was about time!

And again Car goes growling for a long distance. Long, long, long.

When he finally stops we are approached by a manperson, who talks and touches paws with Bill and Marjolyn. I don't know him and strangely enough he talks all kind of different words that I have never heard before. Another type of persons language.

Marjolyn and Bill all of a sudden also speak in this other personslanguage. I am not amused, because now I cannot understand anything at all. I have no idea what's up.

Marjolyn and the manperson go to a territory and Bill and I go back into Car. We go somewhere else without Marjolyn. Curious.

This is not such a long trip and when Car stops, we have arrived at a very large personhouse. My things and my House are coming out of Car and also Bill's and Marjolyn's things.

We are going inside a territory and Bill puts my House and my soft place somewhere, so that I can get into my House. I am safe in my House and I take a good look around to see what happens next.

When Bill has brought all our things into this new territory, we are leaving for a walk together. It is nice but there are no woods and I am kept on my leash. There are many persons walking around and many shiny beasts. All strange streets however.

The persons speak with words that I do not recognize at all. If this goes on I shall have to return to the dog school and start all over again.

Fortunately Bill still talks to me with the words I know. At least that is something.

When the dark comes, we go back to the large personhouse and into the territory. Marjolyn is there as well and she has prepared my dish and my food and drink. Very good.

After my meal I am going into my House and the door is closed.

Marjolyn and Bill are leaving and I am all alone in this new territory. It takes a long time and I am a bit sad, because I don't see anybody at all and I don't even hear them. I start to cry and bark a bit to make myself heard. Maybe somebody will come to pick me up.

It works, because after some crying Bill comes into the territory and he is angry. It is shame on me again...

Why doesn't he understand that I am complaining about this treatment?

We are not going with Car that day and Bill and Marjolyn are going to sleep on a soft place that is also in that territory. I am in my House, but at least they are with me now.

When the light time comes we are going for a walk and upon our return my dishes and food are ready for me. Just the way I like it best.

After the meal I am taken along to the persons' foodplace.

I stayed down close to the paws of my persons and I waited quietly. This meant a treat and this time I got an apple. I have finished it completely.

All our things went back in Car and we have been in Car for a very long time.

I was very happy to be back in our own territory with my Joy-Cat and that other person language was not for me at all. I prefer my own words.

Salt water

Again a day with Car activity. The weather is not too good, because there is a lot falling from the sky and there is much wind. But we are going nevertheless.

My things are not coming along, just a few cookies.

Car stops growling and we get out. What an awful weather. It is raining Cats and Dogs. Not my favorite sort of thing.

Walking on the leash towards an inside territory, where many persons are sitting and, great fun, many dogs of my own type.

All of a sudden I can see the manperson of the trimming, but he doesn't have the trimming table, so I trust nothing of that kind is going to happen to me.

Some of the dogs are behaving stupidly and make fools of themselves and just want to show of that they are mandogs. Others are quite friendly.

I behave properly and take a good look around.

The persons are going to have a meal. The dogs, no way. Not even a cookie is being supplied.

When the persons have finished everybody starts to move and we go to the outside territory. The weather is still bad and I truly hope that it will be a short trip.

My wishes are not fulfilled and after a while my hairs are becoming very wet.

It is no fun at all because we are in a group and on the leashes. No running or romps or playing around.

Charley on the beach

At a certain moment my leash is taken of and we are walking on the sand. I start to run around, down from a hill. I do that many times in our own woods. That's very nice. I can run up and down hill many times.

Now it goes down and when I have arrived, there is a very large sandplace and at the end of this sandplace there is water. A big big waterplace. The water place is so big that you cannot see the end of it.

Another welsh is running around and I approach him to say hello. That is a disappointment, because he doesn't behave friendly at all. He bites. The false guy.

Bill calls me and I am happy with his intervention, because now I can beat a hasty retreat while keeping up the appearances. So no fighting, because the boss calls and that is more important.

Bill has brought my ball along, so we in for some running and romping.

My ears fly in the wind and all of a sudden I couldn't care less that there is so much water dropping from the skies.

Bill throws the ball in the direction of the big water. That water is very strange because it moves and comes towards me. I have never seen that before.

It is quite creepy. I run away and my ball stays behind.

From a distance I take a good look what this is all about. The water goes back and I can get my ball back, because it stayed in the same place.

I get my ball and run to the other side in hopes that Bill will not throw the ball towards the water.

Besides that, I can tell you, that water is absolutely filthy. I was thirsty and wanted to have a drink. Well, no way. Undrinkable.

That day I did not have another drink in that territory. I refused to do it. Not even when we went back to the persons'foodplace. I just didn't trust it. When we were back in our own territory I drank my own water from my own dish. It tasted wonderful.

But I have to say this. I do want to go back to this big sandplace.

162

My things

Marjolyn and Bill have many things, but fortunately I have some property as well.

There are things I like very much, but also some things that belong to me, but that I don't like at all.

The nice things are my Rope and my ball. Stick in the woods is also nice but it doesn't really belong to me, because it is never the same one.

Other nice things are my House and my soft place, my dishes for the food and drink. The nicest thing of all is the box of my cookies. To my utmost regret I can never reach that box myself. I always have to wait for Bill or Marjolyn.

Another box that always stands close to my House contains other things, but some of those I would prefer never to see again.

Tara's collar is okay, but in my opinion everything for the trimming can stay in that box forever.

163

And what about the stinking hissing thing I got from Karen. That has to stay in that box forever and ever.

The box also contains squeaking unreal animals, but I never get them. They belong to me, but they don't give them to me. What a pity because I would reduce them to small pieces with great pleasure.

Since a few light and dark times the box also contains a very new and awful stinking stuff. If they rub that into my hairs, I am at my wits end. I am deeply ashamed to be in the neighborhood of other dogs, because they look at me with pity and that is quite correct.

The worst of the worst is that something comes out of this box that I really hate so much that it makes me cry. They splash in on my hairs and Bill rubs it in thoroughly. The awful smell lingers and lingers. Not even a flea wants to approach me. Even they avoid that dreadful smell.

Can you see and imagine all my friends in the woods looking and sniffing at me. It makes my tail drop into the lowest possible position.

Eating with a fork

Sometime it's a dog's life, although I don't want to complain at all about my situation. I am very happy with my persons.

But, of course, they are just persons, who sometimes haven't the faintest idea what is good for a Welsh.

Take for example the eating of some fruit.

In the morning time Bill prepares some fruit for Marjolyn. Sometimes she drinks it and I don't get anything, because I don't like that sort of drink.

Sometimes the fruit is cut into small pieces and served in a dish.

There are different types of fruits. I don't know the names, but they all taste very well. Sometimes it has a color, sometimes not. I couldn't care less. I love it all.

So, when I see Bill taking the fruit to Marjolyn's everydayplace, I run after him, so that I don't miss it.

For a long time everything went well and I was always given a few morsels that I could eat from Marjolyn's paw.

165

MARJOLYN POLS

Since a few light and darks things have changed.

Persons use their mouth to gobble up their food, but they cannot eat without using their paws. Besides that they use a sort of small stick. The stick picks up the food and takes the food to the mouth.

For the life of me I cannot understand why they should do that, but okay that's persons' manners.

So since some time Bill gives the small stick to Marjolyn to pick in her fruit. I now know that such a stick is called Fork.

Charley learns some table manners

Well, you can feel it coming. I also eat with Fork. I cannot take it into my own paws, but Marjolyn serves me my fruit with Fork.

In the beginning I was too hasty and the fruit fell down on the ground. Nowadays Marjolyn says: "Charley, easy" and then I know that I have to very careful to take Fork into my mouth.

I have become quite good at it and enjoy my fruit. Fortunately none of my friends has ever seen this. I don't want to know what they would think of me.

My persons think I am a clever and good boy and I find that very important. That's why I do all those things. It makes our lives quite comfortable.

Yes, indeed, we have a wonderful life together.

Marjolyn says that I have to stop chatting. Okay, no problem.

Charley's favorite recipes

Breakfast:

Crocks with string beans.

Take 60 grams of my favorite crocks and add some water. Cook 30 grams of string beans in the right way and add these to the other ingredients. Add some more water and ...dinner is ready.

Charley eats his dinner

Crocks with string beans and egg (the recipe for the Differentdays).

As for the previous recipe, but now add a 5 minutes boiled egg in small morsels.

Snacks:

All sorts of fruit, except for the yellow stick, are my favorite snacks. Mostly eaten with Fork.

Lunch menu:

Leftover treat from Bill:

A great selection. For example a piece of bread and butter and cheese. Piece of bread and butter and sausage. A little red ball. A piece of the green stick. And many more. Practically speaking I like everything.

Cocktail snacks:

What is that supposed to be? I just get some crocks from my own food whereas the persons eat all kind of tasty things! I don't drink cocktails anyhow.

Little red balls:

Wash the balls in cold water and dry them with some paper or cloth. Serve in a dish or with paw.

Green sticks:

Wash the green stick and clean it thoroughly. Don't peel. Cut into pieces. I cannot get enough of it and apply myself to it with great pleasure.

Dinner:

Just the same as breakfast.

Some broth is a welcome addition and improves the taste of this dish.

My dictionary

Shiny beast	Car
Round things that roll	Wheels
No	Something that is not allowed or no good
Territory	House or area
Soft place	Bed
Ball	Ball
Outside territory	Kennel or area to play or be outside
Outing	Daily walks
Hug	Hug
Territory with trees	Woods
Flying animals	Birds
Flying animals that walk	Chicken
Everydayplace	Office or sitting room
Makefoodplace	Kitchen
Throwawaythingsbox	Dustbin

Flash and noise thing	TV
Noise thing	Radio
Flash	Camera
Differentday	Sunday or holiday
Struggle	Swim
Sitting place	Sitting room
Coil	Electricity wire
Light and dark times	Days and nights
Stick	Stick
Letgo	Let go
Rope	Rope
Small shiny beast	Vacuum cleaner
Lightmaker	Lamp
Nice noise	Singing
Noise with hands	Hand clapping
Nice noise with voice	Laughing
Green stick	Cucumber
Little red balls	Cherry tomatoes
Grumblebox	Washing machine
Waterbox	Dishwasher

MARJOLYN POLS

About the Author:

Marjolyn Pols started writing stories at the age of six and even published a handwritten girls club magazine!! Won a first prize at primary school at the age of ten. Member of the editing committee for several magazines and responsibilities to fill the gaps in these magazines, made writing stories a daily must.

In the pursuit of quite another career (Export manager for some international companies and traveling all over the world) writing was restricted to business related items for a long time.

Her later involvement in local politics and the need to prepare clear and people oriented presentations, made writing a daily activity again.

Love for animals and this special dog called Charley, plus spare time spent at airports waiting for yet another flight to catch, are the cause of the creation of a series of short stories.

Charley himself, of course is the real author of the book.

Printed in the United States
1252800003B/112

9 781403 381811